Making It in the City

Making It in the City

A Girl's Guide to Starting Life on Your Own in a Ridiculously Expensive City You Can't Afford

Adina Kalish Neufeld

M. Evans and Company, Inc.
New York

M. Evans and Company, Inc.
216 East 49th Street
New York, NY 10017
www.mevans.com

Library of Congress Cataloging-in-Publication Data

Neufeld, Adina Kalish.
Making it in the city : a girl's guide to starting life on your own in a ridiculously expensive city you can't afford / Adina Kalish Neufeld.
    p. cm.
 Includes index.
 ISBN 1-59077-084-6
1. Young women--Life skills guides. 2. City and town life. 3. Finance, Personal. I. Title.
HQ1229.N474 2005
646.7'0084'22--dc22

                    2004030221

Designed and typeset by Chrissy Kwasnik

Printed in the United States of America

9 8 7 6 5 4 3 2 1

Contents

PART THREE: SPARE TIME

Acknowledgments

You'd think a book about making it on your own wouldn't have an acknowledgment section. On the contrary. Yes, most of the work (both the writing and the actual work of getting to the writing) was solitary, but I couldn't have done it without the support of so many individuals. First, to the hundreds of women who shared their own experiences making it on their own, including my friends and family, thank you. Your stories and advice are much appreciated. A special thanks to all of the experts who agreed to share their infinite wisdom: Judith Beck, Ph.D., director of the Beck Institute for Cognitive Therapy and Research, and clinical associate professor of psychology in psychiatry at the University of Pennsylvania; Gene Blumberg, certified public accountant; Bruce Felton, writer; Judith Felton, certified social worker and psychoanalyst; Scott Kays, certified financial planner and president of Kays Financial Advisory Corporation; Karen McGee, director of the Newhouse Career Development Center at Syracuse University; Eric Preston, handyman extraordinaire; Karen Schaeffer, certified financial planner and president of Schaeffer Financial; and Samantha Rifkin, financial analyst, private wealth management, at Goldman Sachs.

I want to express my sincere gratitude to Madelyn Larsen for believing in my work and to Chris Tomasino for helping me launch the original concept of this book. A hearty thanks to my research assistants: Allison Knab and Holly Myers, both of whom are survival gurus in their own expensive towns. Thanks also to Matt Harper at M. Evans, for his infinite wisdom and suggestions, and to Mary Boughton for sharing her ideas. To my family (all over the country), thank you for your motivation and support, and specifically to my brothers, Michael and Alex, who are an endless source of creativity and so many laughs.

Most importantly, I want to thank my husband, Kenny, who is my best friend. For reading numerous drafts at all hours and sharing in all of the highs and lows along the way, a girl couldn't ask for a better (or better-looking) guy. Of course, words cannot begin to describe my feelings for my daughter, Talia, who reminds me on a daily basis that there's so much more to life than work. I hope you'll always strive to pursue your own dreams, even if it means being a little uncomfortable every now and then.

Lastly, I want to thank everyone who has ever said "no" to me. You've given me more inspiration than you'll ever imagine.

Ph.D. in Stress

They say it's supposed to be the best time in your life . . . your twenties into your thirties. But who are they anyway? Youth is one thing, knowing what you're doing with your life and where you're doing it is another. All of a sudden you're supposed to be a responsible adult, balancing a career and your finances, while at the same time trying to find your soul mate? Not to mention having to answer everyone's annoying questions about your plans. And what if you don't want what's "right for you" anyway? Debt, health insurance, moving, networking, chasing your dreams, staying sane! It's more than a little overwhelming if you ask me.

Truth is, life is pretty hard at 20 and 30. They don't know because they're not you. But now's the time to jump in head-first, make mistakes, figure out what you want and how you're going to get it. And with the tips you get here, you'll be well on your way to making it wherever you wind up.

How to Use This Book

Making *It in the City* is a book for women who are in the process of figuring it all out. Maybe you're thinking of moving to a city but don't know if you can afford it. Maybe you've toyed with the idea of opening a business but don't know where to start. You may be single or dating, you may have a job or be unemployed, but what you share with thousands of others right now is that you're embarking on something on your own: life. And wouldn't it be nice to have a little extra help along the way?

Let this book be your best friend. Use it, consult it, rely on it—even yell at it every now and then. It's a resource guide, so you don't have to read it cover to cover. Throw it in your purse and read it on the train on your way to a job interview or when you're looking for an apartment. Take notes in the margins and add your own list of deals and finds. The tips come from my own experiences "making it in the city," as well as from hundreds of women doing the same in expensive and challenging cities all over the country.

You'll find the resource sections heavy on cities like New York, Chicago, San Francisco, and Los Angeles, simply because they're some of the toughest places to live from a financial perspective. And believe me, countless hours of research went into these sections. The apartment listings alone could easily save you a few thousand dollars! So make sure you highlight the resources at the end of each chapter; they'll make your life a lot easier.

Even if you don't live in a really expensive city, there are plenty of resources listed for you, too, to give you a basis for comparison. Of course the advice, how-to sections, and life-changing tips apply to everyone, no matter where you are. And just to give you an added boost of confidence, you'll find true stories of women who've made it on their own—in business, creative careers, and more—with nothing but determination (and a very good sense of humor). Their stories are highlighted in the "*VICTORY!*" sidebars throughout the book.

Hey, nobody said starting out on your own is easy, but you might as well get as much advice as possible from those who've already been there, don't you think?

Preface

I knew I was doomed when I saw the toilet in the kitchen. Literally. It was sitting in the middle of the room next to the fridge. I assumed it wouldn't stay there forever based on the fact that there was a wrench and a plunger (was the guy fixing it planning to actually use it?) lying right next to it. The next apartment had a shower stall in the hallway. Like I was supposed to get naked and march out with my soap with the pizza man at the door? I counted fourteen dead roaches in the third place. You'd think the broker would have at least done a quick sweep-through before bringing in the clients. But this was New York City. You take what you get. Many times sight unseen. And you're supposed to pay the broker 15 percent of your annual rent as a fee to get it. What a joke.

Someone warned me it'd be a challenge to live in New York City. My parents didn't get it. A few people told me I was nuts for going there when there were so many other cities that were so much cheaper. They weren't kidding. All those movies where Meg Ryan is tucked away so comfortably in her cozy brownstone with a quaint fireplace and room for two night tables, plus a wicker trunk? Where was that place?

But I was determined. After huffing and puffing my way up five flights of stairs to the fifth apartment of the day, only to find there were "no drawers in the kitchen," but "plenty of room in the bathroom to keep your forks and knives!" I told my broker to take a hike. Because there was absolutely no way I was going to pay this chump $1,950 *plus* a fee for the dump he was trying to rent me. "You'll never get anything for under $2,000 on your own that's nicer than this!" he shouted on his way down the street, already on his cell phone racing to meet someone else.

"You don't know me very well!" I yelled back. That was the end of my apartment broker experience.

Backpack, notebook, and pen in hand, I proceeded to walk into every single building I could squeeze myself into for the next six hours, asking maintenance people, doormen, and neighbors if they knew about any available apartments. I did this for three days straight, rain or shine. Most laughed, some were actually friendly but had no information, and a few wouldn't say a word until I gave them five dollars. But then I hit the jackpot in the form of a building with a ridiculously nice lobby on 91st Street and Columbus Avenue staffed by a pleasantly plump doorman who was definitely in the mood for a cream cheese fudge brownie, which I just happened to have in my bag.

It worked. He took mercy on me and told me about someone on the third floor who was considering—but not 100 percent sure—about renting his place, his really nice one-bedroom with a modern kitchen. I waited for a minute, thinking there was a catch. There wasn't. So before the doorman even had time to take some paper from the drawer so I could write my name down, I was already upstairs leaving my own note.

By ten o'clock that evening, the owner called me. I was back there at 10:03. The place was incredible. And because I was there at the right time and had some money saved up, it was mine if I wanted it—kitchen drawers and all—for $1,400. I took it.

My roommate conveniently showed up after the hard work was over, but together we built a pressure wall in the living room, turning our cozy one-bedroom into a two. We kissed our common area goodbye and settled in, relishing the fact that our shower and toilet were each in the right place, for $700 each.

I had just passed my first test of living in the most expensive city in the world. And for anyone who's ever lived in New York, you know exactly what I'm talking about.

Part 1

Living

Keeping House

Finding your first place,
then actually living in it

O kay, so I really had no business moving to New York City after graduating from college. With no job, no place to live, and not one contact, I'm not exactly sure what I was thinking. But maybe the fact that I wasn't thinking was how I survived. New York to me was a test—the ultimate challenge—where the rich people lived and where I was going to be like them. Yeah, I know, I've seen every other bright-eyed kid get off the bus thinking she's gonna be a star, but I wanted my shot, too.

After assessing the competition, facing the onslaught of rejection (both personally and professionally), and actually getting a couple of *yes*es along the way, eventually I realized that it wasn't about being a star at all. It was just about being there, on my own, without anyone telling me what to do or how to do it. This in itself was hard enough. With no immediate family nearby, I never felt so petrified and liberated at the same time. Some days really sucked. And the good days were simply those that didn't suck.

Sound familiar? I'm with ya. Growing up hits you like a ton of bricks. One day you're running around without a care in the world. The next thing you know, your parents are moving to Boca and you're supposed to figure out what to do with your life.

Moving Out

Growing up means many things to many people, but mostly it's about taking charge of you. One of the fastest ways to kick that process into gear is to move out on your own. Don't get me wrong, living with your parents to save money is sometimes a necessary means to an end. But sooner or later you're going to have to kiss your Snoopy sheets goodbye. Assuming you're physically able to care for yourself and you're ready to take that big step, this chapter's for you.

Your First Apartment

Looking for your first place can be a daunting experience. There's a lot to consider, especially if you're on a tight budget or you're not sure where you want to live. For those considering a move to a place like New York, Los Angeles, or Chicago, it can really be scary, especially if you don't have a job. Maybe you'll need a roommate. Yeah, yeah, I know. You already did that in college. Well, there are ways to make this experience a little less "sorority-like," shall we say. You know, no more couches on the porch or communal showers. While it may not be the most enticing option, getting a roommate is a great way to save money. The tricks to keeping your lives separate will follow later in the chapter.

Choosing Your City

If you're looking to move somewhere exciting but don't have a clue where to go, check out some of the cities listed at the end of the chapter. Here, you'll find some of the most expensive and difficult ones to conquer (in addition to some other good choices for rent comparison), with info on how to get a deal without getting taken for a ride. The resources can help you get started, and they're mostly free. You can also compare salaries in different cities and find lots of other useful moving information by logging onto www.homestore.com. For more personal advice on different cities, log on to www.fodors.com and click on the "Talk" section. Here, you'll get candid recommendations from people around the globe on everything from travel tips and dining to traffic and cost of living in a particular city. Another fun site is www.findyourspot.com and clicking on "Moving" section. You'll answer a host of questions about what you like and what you're looking for in a city. In turn, you'll get an extensive listing of places tailored to you!

So, Where Do I Begin?

Since each city offers its own excitement and challenges, it's best to do your research ahead of time. If you were lucky enough to get a new job with an employer who's willing to pick up the tab on your move, your expenses and a real-estate agent will be thrown into the deal. If you've decided to move to someplace new just for the experience, or you're embarking on your acting career, you won't be set up with squat. No matter where you decide to move, you should visit first and spend some time combing through the town. If you can stay on a friend's couch, do it. If you don't know a soul, try calling the Y and asking about temporary accommodations. Maximize your time by getting up early. You'll get the most information about apartments by walking around and into buildings, talking to doormen and asking the dog-walking neighbors. Take a notebook, hop on the public transportation. Drive around or pound the pavement. You'll be surprised at how much you can actually learn about the area this way. Here are some other tips to help get you started:

- Contact management companies Management companies generally operate large buildings, several in one city. By contacting the management company directly, you'll avoid the middlemen— the apartment brokers who charge a fee. Typically, the fee ranges from one to two months' rent in cities like Boston, New York, and San Francisco. Before you go to the brokers, try a Google search under "Apartment Management Companies" in your city and see what comes up. The often-neglected phone book is another good resource. And every now and then, while you're walking around, look up: management company names and phone numbers are sometimes listed on the buildings themselves. I've included listings for several cities at the end of the chapter.

- Don't buy no-fee rental lists There are also some companies who'll try to capitalize on your naiveté by selling lists of what they claim are "no fee apartments." While a few places on the list may be legit, the majority of them will be outdated or completely incorrect. You'll lose your $300 and won't have anything to show for it. Whatever you do, don't get suckered into buying these lists.

- Contact your college alumni association Alumni love helping alumni. It's just one of those things. Send an email to your local alumni association asking if anyone knows of an available apartment in town and see what happens. You might get lucky.

- Pray You don't really have to do this, but if you attend a church, temple, or synagogue, post a sign on the bulletin board. Your mother will feel better about it, too, thinking you'll meet a nice guy while you're there.

- Look on Craigslist This is one of my all time favorite websites. It lists no-fee apartments, many by owners themselves, in major cities all over the country. It has a great job board too. See for yourself at www.craigslist.org. In cities that don't charge fees (and are more spread out), you'll also have luck using www.rentnet.com.

- Consider house-sitting or working as a nanny This is a fantastic way to score a place to live, especially for a short time while you're getting stared in a new city. Start by looking through bulletins from your local community center. Or ask around if anyone needs a pet or plant sitter while they're on vacation.

Bottom line: When it comes down to getting a good deal on an apartment, the networking tactics discussed in chapter 3 apply. It's always about being in the know. And the more people you know, the better chance you'll have to get a place.

Things to Look Out For

Before you sign on the dotted line, make sure you do a thorough walk-through of the apartment. It's easy to get carried away, especially when the managing agent is standing over you telling you how lucky you are because there are five other people waiting outside who want this place. Look around and take note of everything. Ask as many questions as you can beforehand. Use the following list as a guide:

- Appliances Are they clean and in working order? Don't be afraid to ask if anything can be replaced. Did you notice a nasty fridge door, a greasy stovetop, a rusty sink? Things like this should be handled before you move in.

- Lights Do they all work?

- Counter space Is there any?

- Faucets This is one that most people overlook. Turn on all the faucets (don't forget the shower). How's the water pressure? You'll be showering here every day (hopefully), so make sure it's decent. Give the toilet a good flush too. Do this with the shower running and see what happens. Your roommate will thank you. You'll probably find a lot of apartments that can't handle both at the same time, but at least you can warn her in advance.

- Closets How many are there? Will the management company let you build another? Is there enough room for a do-it-yourself armoire?

- Windows Do they open and close well? If you're on a bottom floor, are there secure bars? In some states this is a requirement.

- Locks How many locks are on the door? Make sure there are at least two, one of which should be a deadbolt. And ask about getting them changed as well. Who knows where those keys have been?

- Electrical outlets and phone jacks Are there enough?

- **High-speed internet access** Is the building wired or is there wireless access? This is especially important if you'll be working from home.

- **Laundry** Where's the closest laundry room or laundromat? Is it well-lit and safe? When is it open?

- **Floors** Do they need resurfacing or sanding? Does the carpet need cleaning? Who pays for this?

- **Walls** Will they be freshly painted?

- **Bathroom** Is it clean? Same goes for the kitchen. Find out if the building will pay for a thorough cleaning job before you move in.

- **Storage** Is there any additional storage in the building? What about a bike room?

- **Fire escape, sprinkler, and smoke and carbon monoxide detector** Older buildings have fire escapes. Newer ones have sprinklers. All should have smoke detectors. These are musts. Make sure you ask if a fire escape route is posted in your apartment or in the hallway. Familiarize yourself with it.

- **Superintendent** How accessible is the building super or maintenance staff?

- **What's it like at night?** If time permits, go back to the apartment at night. Check out the block, the lighting, and the pedestrian traffic. It's important that you feel comfortable at all times.

- **Who else has lived there?** While you'll always get a mixed bag of responses from previous tenants, it's worth asking what others' experiences have been in a particular building. Questions like "Is the management company responsive?" or "Does the complex attract a certain age group?" will help you get a better feel for the building. A good place to find some candid reviews of apartments is at www.apartmentratings.com.

Beating the Competition

Once you've found something you like and it fits your budget, be prepared to move on it. The more competitive the market, the faster you have to act. If you're planning to move to New York or San Francisco, plan on looking for an apartment no more than one month in advance. And make sure you show up with all the right documents in hand. These include a current letter of employment, pay stub, bank statement, picture ID, tax returns (if you're self employed), and liquid assets (read: cash). Liquid assets will be used to pay your first and last month's rent, as well as security deposit (not to mention your broker's fee if you got suckered into paying one). If you don't have any liquid funds (or, in cities like New York, if you don't make a certain amount to prove you can cover your annual rent), you're going to need a local guarantor or co-signer to help you out. A guarantor is just that—someone who will guarantee that your rent will be paid each month. Being prepared makes the difference between getting a place and not getting one. Most landlords won't even begin to process an application until all of the financials (everything listed above) are presented. So, if you're moving to a highly competitive real estate town, make sure you bring these documents to every appointment you make.

And one last thing: don't dress like a slob when you go to see an apartment. It makes a bad impression, and you may lose a place because you don't look as serious as the next person.

Legal Jargon

Apartment leases can be tricky, so make sure you read yours over very carefully. If you have a legal friend, fax it over to her for a quick look. Again, the more competitive the market, the more the landlords will try to get away with. In many cities you won't have much, if any, room to revise the lease, but making yourself aware of your lease's restrictions will save you time and anxiety later. For example, make sure you find out the penalty for breaking your lease if you have to move out early. Will you simply lose your security deposit (generally one month's rent) or will you be forced to continue to pay rent until your lease is up? Are you allowed to sublet? How much will the rent go up after a year? What about pets? These little snags can mess up your entire living experience if you don't know the answers beforehand. For more information, pick up a copy of *Renter's Rights: The Basics* by attorneys Janet Portman and Marcia Stewart, Nolo Press. It's one of the best no-nonsense guides to help renters like you. You can also log onto www.rentlaw.com and choose your state for specific information on landlord–tenant laws. In New York City, another good resource for tenants is www.tenant.net. In California, download the online guide "California Tenants— A Guide to Residential Tenants' and Landlords' Rights and Responsibilities" from www.dca.ca.gov/legal/landlordbook.

Buying vs. Renting (A Few Quick Words)

With interest rates lower than normal, the average age of a first-time buyer has dropped considerably. So, if you live in a city that's relatively affordable, do a mortgage calculation on www.bankrate.com to see if you're better off buying than renting. With tax deductions offered as incentives for first-time buyers, you'd be surprised at how little a difference there is between a mortgage and a rent.

Now, if you live in New York City, that's a whole different ballgame. In order to buy an apartment in Manhattan, no matter how great your credit is, you're going to have to put down at least 20 percent for your down payment, which is next to impossible for someone making $35,000. Even if you can do that, most apartments for sale in the city are co-ops (short for cooperatives), meaning they're owned by the tenants themselves. Anyone who wants to buy in has to endure a co-op board interview. This process has been compared to being dragged through a car wash hair first and still coming out dirty. The point is, you can spend your entire year putting together an amazing package (consisting of bank statements, tax returns, employer information, credit check, lists of everything you own, extensive letters of recommendation, plus more), spend who knows how much making copies at Kinkos, and impress the heck out of the board president, but if you owe even a nickel to your local grocer, you won't pass and you won't be able to buy in. Do I sound bitter?

So, a personal word of advice: unless you're rich, unless you're lucky and can find a condominium (which has different bylaws than a co-op) that doesn't require you to sign your life away (or you don't care that you'll have to sign your life away), then beware! Now, if you plan on staying in New York City for at least five years and you have the resources, go for it! Just think about the process beforehand so you don't wind up in over your head. But remember, as hard as it is to buy a place in NYC, it's going to be just as hard to sell. Another option for New York is to consider the other boroughs. You'll get more apartment for your money and you may not have to jump through as many hoops to live there.

Mortgages

No matter where you live, you'll need to do research to get the best deal on a loan. Generally, you'll either take a fifteen- or a thirty-year mortgage. The main difference is that with a fifteen-year mortgage you'll pay a higher monthly payment but less interest. A thirty-year mortgage will allow you to spread your payments out over a longer period of time, but you'll wind up paying more in interest. If you really want to save, ask about interest-only mortgages. Your monthly payment will consist purely of interest, but that's how you can get a really low rate. A great place to start your mortgage research is by logging on to www.lendingtree.com. You'll have more banks compete for your business than you'll know what to do with. One word of caution: Whenever a potential lender quotes you a rate, he checks your credit, and so your credit score will go down. This happens with every single lender when you're shopping around. So even if you have perfect credit, watch out, because a low credit score means you won't get the best rate on your mortgage. Only ask for a quote from reputable agencies. If you don't have the time to do your own research, I suggest going through a mortgage broker. You'll pay for the service (fees are wrapped into closing costs, so don't be fooled if they tell you it's free!), but you'll get a better deal without doing any of the legwork. Also, make sure you have the following on hand when you interview lenders: employment information, Social Security card, information on income and debts, current address, type of property you're looking to buy, purchase price, down-payment information, and liquid assets. Once you find a property, you'll also need to get homeowner's insurance.

Once You're In the Place

Whether you're renting or a first-time homeowner, congrats! You got a place! Nice work. Remember, your first few weeks will likely cost you the most as a result of your start-up costs. You'll need to have money for moving expenses, security deposit, phone and cable hook-ups, cleaning supplies, and your first trip to the grocery store. Prepare to shell out at least $300 (more for a house) a week for the first month. It just happens that way. Also, don't forget to fill out a change-of-address form so everyone knows where to find you.

For those living in high-rise buildings with a staff, you'll also need to spend a bit extra tipping your doorman and building superintendent—somewhere around $20 to both—as soon as you move in. As annoying as it is, do this immediately to ensure you'll get good service throughout your stay in their building. If you don't have the cash to do this, give 'em $10 each and bake some cookies.

Construction

If you're lucky enough to get your own place, you rule! If you're stuck living with a roommate but can only afford a one-bedroom apartment, you're going to need a little privacy. One of the best ways to cut the cost of your $2,200 one-bedroom apartment in half is to literally cut your apartment in half. You can do this by hiring a handyman (or handywoman) to build a pressure wall in the living room. This is a wall that's designed to leave the existing walls intact. It can be taken up and down so you don't scar the apartment. Sometimes you can get lucky and find an apartment that already has one up. In New York City, look for apartments in Murray Hill or on the Upper West Side (in the 90s). Otherwise, expect to spend around $1,500 or more to have someone put up a pressure wall in your place. Make sure to ask your handyman to make a window in the wall to allow for better air circulation. You can even hang curtains to make it feel like a real room. It's best to use a licensed contractor in case of damage, and check with the landlord, too.

Making the Most of Your Space

Roommate or not, it's important to make any space feel like home. You can do this without spending a lot of money and still feel like you've left dorm life behind. The following is a list of unique little tips and projects that don't require a Ph.D. (Phat Decorator) and just might do the trick, especially if you're in a small space:

- Buy peel-and-stick tiles These sell for approximately $.50 a square and are a cinch to put over your cheesy linoleum floor. Buy them at any hardware store or Home Depot and they'll spruce up your kitchen. Try the black and white ones in the classic chessboard pattern for a trendy retro, look. They also make peel-and-stick carpet squares in all kinds of funky colors; they look great in the living room or bedroom. You'll find all kinds of modular flooring at www.interfaceflor.com. You can take them up with mineral spirits when you're tired of them—but prepare to spend some time doing it.

- Invest in multipurpose furniture Don't just get a coffee table, get a coffee table that can actually store stuff inside (or use a trunk). In fact, do this for everything you buy. Try to find furniture with doors. It'll keep your apartment from looking cluttered and dusty.

- Buy fold-down tables For small spaces, these can't be beat. Crate and Barrel, Homegoods, Wal-Mart, Target (my personal favorite), Marshalls, T.J. Maxx, Straight from the Crate (NYC), and World Market all carry these small fold-outs with little stools that can be stored underneath. Hide it in the corner when you're done eating.

- Raid your grandmother's attic Antique trunks, old lamps, vintage linens—these items are priceless and are probably collecting dust somewhere in Florida. Ask your grandmother (or any other relative over the age of sixty-five) if she has anything to donate to your new digs. You'll come away with some truly unique items.

- Slip into slipcovers Remember that ratty couch you stole off the porch of the Pi Beta Phi house? Get it steam cleaned. Do this before doing anything else. Then, invest in a slipcover (try www. surefit.com for some unusual patterns). You'll save yourself a few hundred bucks and won't have to think about how many people actually slept on that thing. . . at once.

- Check out space-saver appliances Small kitchen? Keep your counters clear by getting space-saver appliances that can be mounted under wall cabinets. Look on eBay or www.overstock. com for this kind of stuff.

- Use under-the-bed boxes and bags Store your seasonal clothing under the bed and you'll open up a whole new world of closet space. If your bed is on the floor, consider getting "Bed Lifters" (Bed Bath and Beyond or Linens and Things carry these) to raise your box spring off the floor to create more space.

- Browse the flea markets and thrift stores Here, you'll find everything from furniture to socks that can save you money when setting up your place. You'll have the best selection of stuff in the early morning, but you'll also have better bargaining power if you wait until the end of the day. Check out the city-specific recommendations at the end of this chapter and in chapter 7 for some great finds.

- Succumb to do-it-yourself furniture One word: IKEA. While not every city has one of these "disposable furniture" stores, if yours does, get there (see store listings at the end of the chapter or log onto www.ikea.com). The stuff is dirt cheap, durable, and actually pretty cute. A couple of IKEA pieces mixed with your other furniture will keep your apartment from looking like a college dorm. They've got great space-saver solutions too. In New York, IKEA even offers free bus service to the New Jersey store. Also try Target, Wal-Mart, or Home Depot for other do-it-yourself furniture. You'll probably spend the afternoon shouting four letter expletives into the 2 x 4s and wonder why there are a million extra screws in the package, but you'll feel good when you're done assembling it. Crank up the tunes while you're doing this and under no circumstances should you answer a phone call from your mother at the same time.

- **Don't mix business and pleasure** If you're going to be working from home, make sure you have an office "area," no matter how small, in a separate part of the room. A desk, a file cabinet, and a place for your computer is a good start. Keep this space clean and organized. Build shelves. Always think vertically. A jelly cabinet can hold files, papers, envelopes, and all sorts of supplies. A decorative screen will do wonders for keeping your sleeping area separate from your pile of papers. Again, try to get furniture with doors so that when your workday is over you won't have to stare at files when you're sitting on your bed.

- **Paint a wall red . . . or any other color** Do this on one wall only to add some spunk to the room. Try barn red, butter yellow, or periwinkle blue (good for the bathroom). You'll need approximately one pint for every 400 square feet of wall space. Don't forget the primer. Then buy some stencils and give yourself a border on top. When you move out, you may have to paint over in white, but if it looks good the next tenant may want to keep it that way.

Necessities and Tools

Any woman living alone needs to be prepared. For what, you may ask? Anything from bugs to boys. Here's a list of some staples to keep on hand, passed on by women making it on their own nationwide:

- **Keep a full tool box** Stocked with scissors, Phillips head and regular screwdrivers, hammer, pliers, wrench, tape measure, nails, picture hooks, glue, and duct tape.

- **Don't forget the bug spray** Little critters love big cities. Roach traps come in handy, too. A broom is also good for getting those creepy-crawlers off the ceiling.

- **Buy mousetraps à la Tom and Jerry** Not the glue kinds. These are the true bona fide mousetraps used with a piece of Swiss cheese (or peanut butter). If you think you have a mouse, tape a plastic bag onto the floor and put the trap in the middle of the bag, so when the mouse is caught, you can just pick up the bag and don't have to touch anything. Then, feel free to scream at the top of your lungs.

- Load up on condoms, tampons, and Advil No roommate? Who you gonna borrow from when you run out? Keep a warehouse supply on hand.

- Get caller ID Anyone living alone should get this. It's easy, and you'll avoid unwanted pests.

- Block your caller ID Just because you see theirs doesn't mean they have to see yours. Protect your number from showing up on other people's caller ID by getting a block (the phone company can do this for you). Also, list your name in the phone book with initials only and no address.

- Get renter's insurance Seems unnecessary, but this could really come in handy if you ever have a problem in your apartment. For a nominal yearly fee, you're fully protected. For a quote in your area, log on to www.monstermoving.com and click on Renter's insurance. Make sure to ask your agent about *loss of use*, in case your apartment is damaged by fire.

Roommates

If you had to slice your apartment in half and put up a pressure wall, chances are you're living with a roommate. Roommates aren't always the easiest people to deal with, but they can help you save money, especially when you're starting out. If you do decide to buddy up, keep some of these tips in mind. They'll make your life a little easier while you're sharing space.

- Get two phone lines This is a must. I can't tell you how many arguments you'll avoid about missed messages or whose voice should go on the answering machine, not to mention the problems that arise when your roommate moves out without paying her last phone bill and *you* get stuck with the choice of paying it or wrecking your own credit rating. The investment will save you hundreds in legal fees (after you've beaten each other up). If you can't afford to do this and don't want to use your cell, then I highly suggest getting a voice-mail service. For about $10 a month, you get a local number and a private outgoing message. Look under *Voice Mail* services in the phone book or ask your local phone provider if they have a service. It's worth it. If you're going to bypass the landline altogether, you might as well get the best deal on a cell phone. For the latest comparisons of cell phones and plans, log on to www.getconnected.com.

- **Make schedules** No, you don't need a chore wheel like in summer camp, but do have an idea who is going to clean and when. Do you both need to be out of the apartment by 7:30 A.M.? If so, consider showering in the evening or going to the gym before work. Little things like this can shave the annoyance off your day when you're waiting by the bathroom door wondering what the *heck* she's doing in there.

- **Decide what you're going to do about food immediately** I hate those people who eat my cereal and then never replace it. Don't let that happen. When you move in, decide right away if you'll be sharing food. If not, pick your cabinets and start stocking up. Farmers' markets are overflowing with cheap produce. You may even consider joining a warehouse club like Sam's Club, Costco, or BJ's, or even joining a food co-op. These wholesome alternatives to big grocery stores often provide fresh produce and food staples at low costs. While they tend to appeal to the "earthier" types, they're worth investigating. If you decide to share food, lay out the ground rules together as a team. The first shopping trip will be your biggest. Load up on pasta, rice, canned goods, frozen dinners, soups, condiments, paper goods, etc. Then split the bill. Afterwards, you may want to set aside one day for shopping. If you can go together, great. If not, make sure you both agree to replace perishables when they're finished. Nobody wants to come home to an empty carton of milk in the refrigerator. Another way to do this is to make a petty cash box. Every week, add $20 to the box and agree to use this cash for necessities only. You'll learn to be more frugal in the grocery store if you have a predetermined limit. If you have a list on the fridge of what's needed, you can take turns going to the store and make sure you stay stocked with the foods you both like. The bottom line when it comes to sharing food is consideration. If it gets to the point where you're the only one pitching in, it's time to have a little talk with your roommate.

- **Don't share furniture** Food is one thing, furniture another. Why? Because when you move out, you'll fight over how much you owe for the couch. Then you'll spend an inordinate amount of time explaining how it's devalued over time. Buy a few pieces for yourself and keep them when you leave. You'll save yourself money in the long run.

- **Know your bounds** Is your roommate uncomfortable with you bringing your dates home? Maybe this is okay twice a month, but every Thursday, Friday, and Saturday? Uh-uh. Decide before you move in what your sleepover rules are so you can both feel at ease. I've heard so many stories about roommates whose boyfriends conveniently moved in without paying rent. And then there were three. The guys weren't *officially* living there, but they might as well have been. So, even if you think you're cool with this, you may not be after a month of finding his boxers on your bathroom floor—especially if you're in a small apartment. Make it clear to your roommate before you move in that boyfriends or girlfriends need their own primary residence. You can even ask for proof of address. Just kidding. The point is this: Try not to turn the place into a frat house. You'll appreciate it when the tables are turned.

- **Know when to call it quits** Having trouble with a roommate who was once your best friend? They say you learn the most about someone once you live with her. If you've given your living situation a fair shot and it's just not working out, maybe it's time to say goodbye before the friendship goes south. Talk to your roommate about alternate living arrangements, such as moving to a larger place with more roommates or splitting up for good. Try not to screw your roommate by finding another place and leaving her to fill your spot. That's just not neighborly. List things on paper that are bothering you. Give her a month or two to see if she's responsive to your gripes. If not, it may just be time to move on.

- **Be flexible** It's not a lifetime arrangement, so recognize that everything won't always be done your way. Try and make the most of your living quarters so that you can actually call your place *home*.

City-Specific Resources

Atlanta

Overview: A very affordable city with lots of action. Great singles' scene, too. You'll have no problem finding a place to live.

Average cost for a 700-square-foot apartment: $800–$850

Areas to check out: Decatur, Brookhaven, Virginia Highlands, Little Five Points, Vinings, Dunwoody, Emory/Briarcliff, Midtown and Buckhead (more expensive); some new areas include Fairlie-Poplar, Poncey-Highlands, Castleberry Hill, Reynoldstown, Cabbagetown, and Grant Park. There are plenty of apartment complexes in Atlanta and most are clamoring for your business, so make sure you negotiate a few months' free rent if you choose one of these bigger complexes.

Apartments

www.freeapartmentlocators.com
770-394-2088

www.homestore.com

atlanta.craigslist.org

Other Start-Ups

Phone, Cable, and Internet

Bellsouth
www.bellsouth.com
888-757-6500

Comcast
www.comcast.com

404-266-2278

Electric

Georgia Power
www.georgiapower.com
404-506-6526

Car

Department of Motor Vehicles
www.dmvs.ga.gov/moving/
A car in Atlanta is pretty necessary, as public transportation isn't as convenient as in some other cities, though it's getting better. You have 30 days from when you move to get your new license and register your vehicle. See the website for offices near you.

Boston

Overview: This city isn't cheap. Generally, you'll find apartment brokers who charge an average of one month's fee just to rent a place. Try to avoid this if possible.

Average cost for a 700-square-foot apartment: $1,600

Areas to check out: Try South Boston, Allston, Brighton, Jamaica Plain, Sommerville, and Cambridge for slightly lower rents.

Apartments

www.starrealtygroup.com
617-731-0955

Alpha Management
www.bostonapartments.com/alpha.htm
(Make sure you type the "alpha" or you'll get a fee-based website.)
617-789-4445

Resource Capital Group
www.rcg-llc.com
617-625-8315

Charles E. Smith Companies
www.smithapartments.com

www.roommateconnection.com

boston.craigslist.org

800-APT-SHARE

Other Start-Ups

Phone, Cable, and Internet

Verizon
www22.verizon.com
800-870-9999

Comcast
www.comcast.com
800-COMCAST

Electric

N Star
www.nstaronline.com
800-592-2000

Car

Department of Motor Vehicles
www.mass.gov/rmv/
Depending on where you live, you may or may not need a car. Public transportation is excellent and commuter trains travel to outlying areas.

Chicago

Overview: Chicago offers a wide variety of apartments and lofts in lots of great areas. Compared to New York City rents, Chicago's a bargain!

Average price for a 700-square-foot apartment: $850+

Areas to check out: Roscoe Village, Andersonville, Ravenswood, Lincoln Square, Bucktown (more expensive), Logan Square (west of Bucktown), Wicker Park, Pilsen, Rogers Park, and Ukrainian Village. Lofts abound!

Apartments

The Apartment Connection
www.theaptconnection.com
1000 W. Diversey
773-525-3888

The Chicago Reader
www.chireader.com

The Apartment People
www.apartmentpeople.com
3121 North Broadway
773-248-8800

Chicago Apartment Finders
www.chicagoapartmentfinders.com
906 West Belmont
773-883-8800

ICM Properties
www.icmproperties.com
773-549-5443

Kass Management
www.kassmanagement.com
2000 North Racine, Suite 3400
773-975-7234

Second City Rentals
www.secondcityrealty.com
1105 West Chicago Avenue, Suite 303
312-850-1316

Jerome H. Meyer Properties
www.jhmproperties.com
312-944-2700
Reasonably priced properties in the Lincoln Park, Wrigleyville, Lakeview, and Old Town areas. Ask about move-in specials—they often offer a free month's rent.

chicago.craigslist.org

Other Start-Ups

Phone, Cable, and Internet

SBC
www.sbc.com
800-244-4444

Comcast
www.comcast.com
800-COMCAST

Electric

Commonwealth Edison Company (ComED)

PECO Energy
www.exeloncorp.com (for both)
800-483-3220

Car

Department of Motor Vehicles
www.cyberdriveillinois.com

Some say they're fine without a car in Chicago; others say you really need it. With many people commuting to the suburbs for work, you may find it's a necessity. Inside the city, public transportation is good and buses are widely used.

Furniture Finds

Wolff's Flea Market
Indoors, 2031 North Mannheim (corner of N. Avenue)
Melrose, IL
847-524-9590
Sundays from 6 a.m. to 3 p.m.

New Maxwell Street Market
Canal Street and Roosevelt Road
Sundays from 7 a.m. to 3 p.m.

Get your flea-market needs met amid some 500 vendors and live blues music.

All Night Flea Market
2015 Manchester Road, DuPage County Fairgrounds
Wheaton, IL
715-526-9769

Once a year extravaganza, every August.

Chicago Antique Market
Randolph Street, between Ada and Ogden
312-951-9939
May to October, last Sunday of each month.

Affordable Portables Lifestyle Furniture
2608 North Clark
773-935-6160
www.affordableportables.net

Cheap, and crammed in every corner of the store are lots of desks, tables, shelving, plus plenty of futons.

Brown Elephant Resale Store
3651 North Halsted
773-549-5943

Gently used furniture.

Roy's Furniture Co.
2455 North Sheffield Avenue
773-248-8522

Great deals on tables, chairs and sofas, with an enormous selection.

Room and Board
55 Ohio Street
312-266-0656
www.roomandboard.com
Very similar to Crate & Barrel, with some good deals on sofas and lots of large-framed prints.

Crate & Barrel Outlet
1864 North Clyborn Avenue
312-787-4775
Lots of cheap extras for kitchen, bathroom, and office, plus the occasional great furniture deal.

CB2
800 West North Avenue
312-787-8329
Crate & Barrel's cheaper, younger sibling, CB2 stocks lots of fun (and sometimes kitschy) apartment décor.

IKEA
1800 East McConnor Parkway
Schaumburg, IL
847-969-9700

Los Angeles

Overview: Sprawling, yes, but that also means more living choices for you. The closer you get to the ocean or the hills, the more expensive the rents. Plan to spend a lot of time in your car. But when you're driving around, don't forget to look up—lots of management companies list their numbers on the buildings themselves, especially in areas like Brentwood and Santa Monica. Something else to know about Los Angeles: many apartments don't come with refrigerators (go figure!). Make sure to ask if yours does.

Average price for a 700-square-foot apartment: $1,250

Areas to check out: Silver Lake, West Hollywood, Westwood, Santa Monica, Manhattan Beach, Pasadena (a bit further out, and not as much in the scene, but very nice)

Less expensive areas include: Long Beach, West Los Angeles, Palms/Culver City, Mid-Wilshire (has lots of apartment buildings), Koreatown, Echo Park, Mount Washington/Highland Park/South Pasadena, and Downtown (undergoing extensive revitalization).

Apartments

www.homestore.com
click on "Apartments"

Westside rentals
www.westsiderentals.com
310-395-RENT
This is a fee-based service. Offices in Santa Monica, Hermosa Beach, Studio City, Hollywood, Pasadena, and Costa Mesa.

Los Angeles Times
www.latimes.com
Online listings updated daily; routed through www.apartments.com.

LA Weekly
www.laweekly.com/classifieds
Print edition comes out on Wednesdays. Online edition updated daily.

The Recycler
www.recycler.com
Print edition comes out on Thursdays. Online edition updated continuously. A very resourceful publication that is under utilized!

"The Original" Apartment Magazine
www.aptmag.com

www.roommatematchers.com

www.roommateaccess.com

losangeles.craigslist.org

Other Start-Ups

Phone, Cable, and Internet

SBC
www.sbc.com
800-310-2355

Adelphia
www.adelphia.com
888-683-1000

Comcast
www.comcast.com
800-COMCAST

Electric

Los Angeles Department of Water and Power
www.ladwp.com
818-342-5397

Car

Department of Motor Vehicles
www.dmv.ca.gov/
Um, yeah. You're gonna need one.

Furniture Finds

Out of the Closet
Locations in Atwater Village, Beverly Hills, East L.A., Fairfax, Hollywood, Long Beach, North Hollywood, Pasadena, South Pasadena, Venice, West Hollywood, and West L.A. Some great bargains can be found at these thrift stores. Check your phone book for local listings.

Further
4312 West Sunset Blvd.
323-660-3601
Sells funky new stuff.

Pasadena City College Flea Market
www.pasadena.edu/fleamarket
1570 East Colorado Boulevard
Pasedena, CA
626-585-7906
First Sunday of every month, 8 a.m. to 3 p.m.

Rose Bowl Flea Market and Market Place
1001 Rose Bowl Drive
Pasadena, CA
323-560-7469
Second Sunday of every month

IKEA
600 N. San Fernando Blvd.
Burbank, CA
818-842-4532
L.A. is also known for its surplus of farmers markets, with fantastic and cheap produce. The Santa Monica market (on Arizona & 2nd Avenue) is the biggest.

Miami

Overview: You shouldn't have too much of a problem scoring an apartment here. You'll get a cheaper place if it's not *right* on the beach, but hey, can't have everything, right?

Average price for a 700-square-foot apartment: $850 (more expensive in South Beach).

Areas to check out: Kendall and North Miami Beach.

Apartments

www.rentmiami.com
877-725-3372

Charles E. Smith Companies
www.smithapartments.com (a bit more expensive)

www.roommateclick.com (a national service)

maimi.craigslist.org

Other Start-Ups

Phone, Cable, and Internet

Bellsouth
www.bellsouth.com
888-764-2500

Comcast
www.comcast.com
800-COMCAST

Electric

Florida Power & Light
www.fpl.com
954-797-5000

Car

Department of Motor Vehicles
www.hsmv.state.fl.us/
Florida is another must-have car state. You'll need one.

New York City

Overview: This one takes the cake for being the most expensive and most difficult city to score a place to live. You have to really use your noodle, as there are very few free resources in NYC. A handful of management companies who don't charge a fee are listed below. The list excludes luxury buildings, which are too expensive for me to recommend in good faith.

Average price for a 700-square-foot apartment: $2,200 (this is not a joke).

Areas to check out: You'll pay top dollar in hot areas such as the Upper West Side, East and West Village, Hell's Kitchen, and Chelsea. Try Hell's Kitchen, Murray Hill, Washington Heights, and Hudson Heights for slightly lower rents. Expand your search to Williamsburg and Park Slope, Brooklyn; Roosevelt Island; Hoboken and Jersey City, NJ; or Astoria, Queens, and you'll get more space for your money.

Apartments

Jakobsen Realty
www.nofeerentals.com
212-533-1300
11 Waverly Place

William Gottlieb (West Village)
558 Hudson Street
212-989-3100

City and Suburban (Upper East Side)
511 East 78th Street
212-517-3000

Harfay Management (Upper East Side)
1641 First Avenue (studios only)
212-570-6174

Pine Management Company (Upper West Side)
212-316-2114

Solil Management Company
212-265-1667

Sky Management
www.nofeeapartments.net
226 East 54th Street, Suite 402
212-759-1300 x22

Bettina Equities Management Company
www.bettinaequities.com
227 East 85th Street
212-744-3330

Ardor New York
www.ardorny.com

This is a broker with a fee but has some good deals anyway, sometimes with no fee.

Manhattan Skyline
www.manhattan-skyline.com
212-408-9447

Keyah (Upper West Side)
www.keyah.com
165 West 73rd Street
212-595-5566

$20 (refundable) plus a business card will get you keys to go check out their apartments.

www.villagevoice.com

www.roommatefinders.com

newyork.craigslist.org

Other Start-Ups

Phone, Cable, and Internet

Verizon
www.verizon.com
212-890-7100

Time Warner Cable
www.twcnyc.com
212-358-0900

Cablevision
www.cablevision.com
718-617-3500

Electric

ConEdison
www.coned.com
800-752-6633

Car

Department of Motor Vehicles
www.nydmv.state.ny.us/reg.htm

Oooh . . . you're asking for it if you have a car. Parking in the city is a nightmare, not to mention the fact that you'll pay the equivalent of another rent if you have to get a garage. Good luck!

Furniture Finds

Greenflea
Columbus Avenue and 77th Street
Sundays 10:00 a.m. to 5:30 p.m. all year

Forget the furniture, don't miss the cider and donuts located at the corner entrance by the plants!

Hell's Kitchen Flea Market
West 39th Street between 9th and 10th Avenue
Saturday and Sunday 9 a.m. to 5 p.m.

Lots of vendors have recently made this cool flea market even bigger.

ABC Carpet
www.abchome.com
Broadway and 19th Street

The place is mucho expensive, but you can get some fantastic decorating ideas. I list it for this reason only. There's also an ABC outlet in the Bronx worth checking out.

Gothic Cabinet and Craft
www.gothiccabinetcraft.com
Locations all over NYC.

If you're willing to finish the pieces yourself, you can actually get a great deal. It'll cost you a bit more if you let them do it for you.

Straight from the Crate
www.straightfromthecrate.com
Locations all over NYC.

Not dirt cheap, but they've got a lot of space-saver options crammed into a small store.

IKEA
Elizabeth Center
1000 IKEA Drive
Elizabeth, NJ
908-289-4488

Take the free shuttle bus from Port Authority bus terminal on Saturdays and Sundays. (There's also an IKEA on Long Island.)

San Francisco

Overview: This one's another toughie. Consider expanding your search to the surrounding areas for a better deal.

Average price for a 700-square-foot apartment: $1700

Areas to check out: Noe Valley, Glen Park, Haight, UCSF, Bernal Heights, Mission, (commuting options for cheaper rent include: Berkeley, San Jose, and Sunnyvale).

Apartments

The Rental Source
www.therentalsource.com
415-771-7685

Affordable Property Management
www.apm7.com
510-487-2583

Ford Real Estate
www.fordrealestate.com
415-824-7200

Litke Properties
www.litkeproperties.com
415-922-0178

Saxe Real Estate
www.saxerealestate.com
415-474-2435

www.roommates.com (a national service)

sanfranciso.craigslist.org

Other Start-Ups

Phone, Cable, and Internet

SBC
www.sbc.com
800-310-2355

Comcast
www.comcast.com
800-COMCAST

Electric

Pacific Gas and Electric
www.pge.com
800-743-5000

Car

Department of Motor Vehicles
www.dmv.ca.gov/

Expensive, but many say it's a necessity, especially if you live in the outlying areas.

Furniture Finds

Ashby Flea Market
Fourth Street and Ashby
to West Berkeley, CA
510-644-0744
Saturdays and Sundays, 7 a.m. to 7 p.m.

San Jose Flea Market
www.sjfm.com
1590 Berryessa Rd.
800-BIG-FLEA
Wednesday through Sunday all day.

IKEA
Emeryville
4400 Shellmound Street
Emeryville, CA
510-420-4532

Seattle

Overview: Not too cheap either, but you can get some good stuff online.

Average price for a 700-square-foot apartment: $1,200

Areas to check out: Freemont and Ballard.

Apartments

www.seattleapartmentfinder.com

www.roommates.com (a national service)

seattle.craigslist.org

Other Start-Ups

Phone, Cable, and Internet

Comcast
www.comcast.com
800-COMCAST

Qwest
www.qwest.com
206-264-4600

Electric

Puget Sound Energy
www.pse.com
206-382-7858

Seattle City Light
www.seattle.gov/light/
206-684-3000

Car

Department of Motor Vehicles
www.dol.wa.gov/
You'll probably need a car here.

Washington, D.C.

Overview: In town, you'll get a decent size space for a decent chunk of change. D.C.'s Metro goes everywhere, so don't be afraid to expand your search to Northern Virginia or parts of Maryland to see if you can get a better deal.

Average price for a 700-square-foot apartment: $1,350

Areas to check out: Northwest D.C., Dupont Circle, Cleveland Park, Woodley Park, Adams Morgan, Mt. Pleasant, Foggy Bottom, U Street, and Capitol Hill. Try Alexandria and Arlington, Virginia, and Chevy Chase, Bethesda, and Silver Spring, Maryland, for slightly more space for your money.

Apartments

Washington City Paper
www.washingtoncitypaper.com

Washington's free weekly lists plenty of housing for rent throughout the
D.C. area, plus housing to share listings.

www.rentnet.com

Charles E. Smith Companies
www.smithapartments.com

washingtondc.craigslist.org

Other Start-Ups

Phone, Cable, and Internet

Verizon
www.verizon.com
202-954-6263

Adelphia
www.adelphia.com
888-683-1000

Comcast
www.comcast.com
800-COMCAST

Electric

Pepco
www.pepco.com
800-424-8028

Car

Department of Motor Vehicles

In D.C.: www.dmv.washingtondc.gov

In Maryland: www.mva.state.md.us/

In Virginia: www.dmv.state.va.us/

D.C. will be the most expensive in terms of keeping a car, but you may
need one, depending on your commute. Public transportation is excellent
and trains travel to all areas.

Furniture Finds

Eastern Market
www.easternmarket.net
7th Street and North Carolina Avenue
Saturdays 10 a.m. to 5 p.m.

You can find everything from jewelry to frames to furniture at this place.

Miss Pixie's Furnishings and Whatnot
1810 Adams Mill Road NW
202-232-8171
Thursdays through Sundays.

Rummage through furniture and tableware picked up by the store's owner at antique stores, and come back often: the turnover here is quick. Upholstered chairs run from $50 to $350 dollars; table and chair sets range from $150 to $250.

Ruff & Ready Furnishings
1908 14th Street NW
202-667-7833
Saturdays and Sundays.

Browse through a range of pre-1950s furniture and accessories in this store's 5,000 square feet of space.

Upscale Resale Shop
8100 Lee Highway
Falls Church, VA
703-698-8100

Find castoffs from lawyers, politicians, and other professionals at this resale shop, plus some new upholstered pieces.

IKEA
2901 Potomac Mills Circle
Woodbridge, VA
703-494-4532

2

~~~~~~~~~~~~~~

Moolah

Getting yours in the right place

One of the most difficult things—maybe *the* most difficult thing about being on your own—is managing your money. And even if you're not doing this 100 percent on your own, you're still going to be managing some of it (such as your daily cash flow, your expenses, your disposable income, etc.) in a way you've never had to do before.

What's important to learn on your own is how to cut back. It doesn't matter how much you make, either. Whether it's $20,000 or $100,000 a year, the key to financial success when you're just starting out is learning to live *below your means*. Yeah, I know! You're young, you're free, you have no mortgage, no kids, and no responsibilities! Why save?

Because, if you do it now, you'll be better off in five years. End of story.

This was a very hard concept for me to grasp. My first job out of college paid $24,000 a year in New York City. I quickly learned that sushi and sake three nights a week, in addition to the rent for my small apartment, wasn't the best way to get my money to compound. I weighed the options. Making my own sushi wasn't one, so I cut back. I stopped shopping for things I didn't need, and I stopped taking cabs. I also went to Starbucks only on Fridays as an end-of-the-week treat. And it worked.

Learning to Budget

So what does living below your means really signify on a larger scale for you? In talking with the experts, most suggest that saving 10 percent of whatever you make will do the trick. Think of it as your own little tithe. In ancient times, 10 percent of income was given to the church as a gift. And while I'm all for donations, at this stage of your life it's best to donate your time and keep your money. I know what you're thinking (because I thought it, too): "How in the world can I save 10 percent of my measly paycheck, which works out to—for example—only $1,409.51 a month, after taxes?" Just pretend there are more taxes taken out and your check sucks even more than it really does.

I'm not saying you should deprive yourself of a fun night out, but don't blow $100 every Friday night and then wonder why you're not saving. Don't buy the new Banana Republic Harrison low-rise slate blue pinstripe pants for $88 and then wonder why you don't have money. But I digress. The point is, starting early will make all the difference in the world. The best way to kick this process into gear is to take control of your spending. Here are some quick and easy suggestions that can help you do this without making you feel like a loser:

- Every now and then, put the four bucks you were going to use for a double decaf mocha no-foam latté into a jar. You'll be amazed at how much you'll save by the end of a year.

- Go to the cheap movie theater instead of the expensive one (there's one in every city).

- Eat dinner at home and then go out for drinks, not both. Or, cook your own feast. See chapter 7 for creative (and cheap) cooking classes.

- Use your debit card instead of your credit card, so money gets immediately deducted from your bank account. You'll be less likely to spend when you see your balance dipping into the double digits (or single ones).

- Buy clothes off-season.

- Suggest doing holiday grab bags with your family so you only have to buy one gift instead of five.

- Avoid going to large dinner parties where everyone splits the check—even though you just ate a salad. It's easier than looking like the cheapo.

- Consider volunteering to be a guinea pig at a fancy hair salon. You'll get a great cut (or color), but you may not always get to pick the style.

- If you have a choice between taxis and public transportation, take public transportation. It's kind of a no-brainer, but sometimes it's easy to forget this.

Are you still with me? Living below your means is a challenge, but every little bit helps. Start by following these suggestions and you'll gradually change your mentality to keep your spending habits under control. Put the money into a savings account until you can afford to open an IRA (individual retirement account) and then have the money automatically deducted from your paycheck so you aren't tempted to do something else with it. Simply build your lifestyle around a reduced income for five years. If you want to be able to draw on this nest egg for a future down payment, keep your money in a liquid account (one where you can withdraw cash with no penalty). Just don't be tempted to use it on tickets to Tahiti!

Mapping Your Budget

What'll really help you control your spending is to set a budget for yourself. Here are some things you'll want to include:

1. Income
2. Rent
3. Utilities
4. Food
5. Transportation/car payments and insurance
6. Gas
7. Cell phone
8. Loans
9. Credit-card debt
10. Gym
11. Restaurants, movies, clubs/leisure activities
12. Airline tickets and travel

Make sure it's realistic. Remember, items 2 through 12 need to add up to *less than* item 1. You'll notice that there are only a few areas you have a lot of control over—if you need to cut back, it's going to be the fun stuff. Sorry. Don't forget to add an additional 10 percent for savings. To do an automated calculation, log on to http://www.bankrate.com/brm/calc/Worksheet.asp.

Setting Up Your Bank

Once you know how much you have to work with, you're going to need a place to put it. I highly advise against storing your cash under your mattress. Instead, try to find a bank that offers free checking, convenient branch locations and ATMs, and weekend or evening hours. Always opt for direct deposit from your employer, too, just to keep from having to make extra trips.

Checking Account

This is something you'll want to get within the first few weeks of moving to a new city. If you're moving with a job, you'll probably get some advice from your employer along with a welcome kit from a bank. But if you're on your own, you'll want to shop around and see which bank offers you the most for less.

Some things to look for: Does the bank require a minimum balance? Does the bank charge a fee if you drop below the minimum balance? Is there automatic *overdraft protection* (an instant loan given to you by the bank if you bounce a check or take out more than what's in your account)? Can you link accounts? Is online banking part of the package? What's the fee if you use a different banks ATMs? How many ATMs/branches do they have in the area? Do they have Saturday banking hours? What other services do they provide? There really is a difference between banks. Make sure you take a look at the suggestions listed at the end of the chapter.

Credit Cards

Most money gurus will tell you to avoid credit cards completely and stay out of credit-card debt. They're right. But man, it's hard. Who can resist the extra 15 percent off at Banana (and Gap, and Benetton, and Abercrombie, and Ann Taylor) when you open a charge? Unfortunately, opening a slew of credit card accounts isn't going to help your credit and you'll likely lose them anyway. What you'll probably need, however, is a Visa, MasterCard, or American Express. American Express offers fantastic customer service, but because vendors have to pay higher fees, it's not accepted everywhere. Just something to keep in mind. As far as Visa and MasterCard go, now that college is over you won't get people yelling at you from tables in the student center with airline vouchers and free mobile minutes if you sign up. But there are plenty of cards out there that offer extras. Do a custom search for the best credit cards to suit your needs at www.bankrate.com

(click on credit cards). Here, you can specify if you need a card with no fee, one with a low *Annual Percentage Rate* (known as APR, this is the amount of interest you pay each month if you don't pay your bill in full), cash back, or any that have perks, and you'll get a detailed listing of a variety of cards.

One word of caution: a credit card offer may sound great on a brochure, but make sure you read the fine print on the back of the application. Many charge fees or have weird little clauses about when you have to pay up. This is especially true for those cards that invite you to "transfer your balance" and "pay nothing for five years!" Also, beware of introductory rates that advertise 0% APR. The fine print will tell you this only lasts three months and then, guess what? You'll be paying late fees *and* a much higher interest rate. I learned this the hard way. If you can, try and pay off your full balance every month. So many people dig themselves deep in debt, a little at a time. Don't be one of them.

Student Loans

If you're going to start paying back any college loans immediately, you probably won't be able to save. But don't fret; getting out of debt is putting you in the right direction. If you have hefty student loans to pay back, now's the time to figure out how to do it and still have money left to pay the rent (and go shopping).

You've probably heard a lot about loan consolidation lately. So what is it? Loan consolidation allows you to combine two or more federal student loans together to give you lower interest rates, lower monthly payments, and the ease of sending in one payment per month instead of several. Before you do this, figure out if it's worth your while. Many consolidation companies will market their services to you as if it's the perfect solution for your money woes. Once you combine your loans, you'll lock in the interest rate for the remainder of the loan period. This can be good or bad, depending on your rate. So do your research to get the best deal. "And," adds financial advisor Karen Schaeffer, "always figure out your budget *before* you decide to restructure your finances so you know what you're working with."

For detailed information on paying back your loans, log on to www.studentaid.ed.gov. For information on loan consolidation, log on to loanconsolidation.ed.gov or www.finaid.org. Karen also recommends www.myvesta.org, a not-for-profit consumer education organization. You'll pay a fee for the advice, but you'll get experts (rather than people just working the phones) who can help you figure out the best option for you.

If you do qualify for federal loan consolidation, you'll have four options:

- Standard repayment plan You pay a fixed monthly amount for ten years.

- Extended repayment plan You pay a fixed monthly amount for twelve to thirty years. Your interest will be higher even though your monthly bill is lower.

- Graduated repayment plan You pay a low amount to start and then gradually increase your payments for a total period of twelve to thirty years. Your monthly payment will increase every two years.

- Income contingent repayment plan As it sounds, your monthly payments will be based on your personal financial situation. You'll have up to twenty-five years to pay back your loan.

No matter how you decide to pay back your loans, make sure to find out if you qualify for a grace period (where you don't have to pay anything for a few years), especially if you consolidate while you're still in school.

Some other words you may want to familiarize yourself with are *loan forbearance* and *loan deferment*. If you have federal loans and you're unemployed, or a full-or part-time student, the government may allow you to defer your loans until you're in a better place financially. If you qualify, the government may also pay back the interest for you. Contact your loan provider to find out. If you are in *loan forbearance*, you can hold off on paying back the loans for a set amount of time, but you'll be responsible for the interest that accrues. Still, while these options may work for you right now, it's always best to try and start paying back your loans as soon as possible.

If you don't even remember what kind of loan you have, log on to the National Student Loan Data System (www.nslds. ed.gov). Here you can search a central database of all Department of Education Loans and use their secure server to access your personal file.

Doing Your Own Taxes

Just the thought makes me cringe. Like you really need to be reminded of your financial status when you're barely paying the rent? Taxes are a drag, but there's no way around them. You might as well take a deep breath and plow through this section.

Generally, if you work full-time for one company and don't have any side jobs or lots of money in different accounts, your taxes shouldn't be too crazy. You'll get a W-2 form in the mail (wage statements from your employer) and you'll need to fill out something called a 1040. If you make less than $50,000, you'll use the 1040E-Z or the 1040A (depending on your income and deductions). In addition to your W-2 forms, you'll get statements in the mail from your bank(s) or investment firm(s) listing interest you've made on your accounts over the past year. These are called 1099 forms. Since this interest is considered income, you must report it to the IRS. The income you get from working (called earned income) combined with income you get from your investments (called unearned income) makes up your *gross income*. You see this term a lot on your income tax returns.

If you're just starting out on your own, you'll likely file under "Single" (Do they really need to remind you of *this* too? Geez!) and take the *standard deduction*. This is an amount of money calculated by the federal government that is deducted from your gross income. The whole concept of a standard deduction is based on the fact that the government knows you've spent money to further your career, make charitable donations, or pay medical bills, so they give you a break in a fixed amount (just under $5,000 for singles). If you spent less than this—making resume copies or doing something else you could deduct—consider yourself lucky, you get a freebie. If you spent more than the standard deduction, you'll probably want to *itemize*. This means you'll have to go through your receipts from the entire year and list out every business-related expense to prove to the IRS that you indeed spent more on job-related things than what the government's giving you.

Things get a lot more complicated when you're self-employed, own your own business, work lots of different jobs, or have money coming in from various channels. In any of these cases, you may need to file separate forms (known as schedules) to reflect income from these sources, be it contract work (for which you'll get 1099 forms from your employers) or dividends in excess of certain amounts. Additional information about schedules for businesses can be found in Chapter 5, but here's a quick rundown of some that may apply to you:

- Schedule A is for itemized deductions.
- Schedule B is for reporting taxable dividends and interest income.
- Schedule C or Schedule CE or SE is for reporting profits and losses from a business.
- Schedule D is for reporting capital gains and losses.

If filing taxes is new to you and you've got income coming in from several different sources, I highly recommend getting an accountant, especially if you're planning on itemizing your expenses. Itemizing can get very nit-picky, as the IRS will want you to categorize your expenses accordingly. Ask around for a referral or stop by an H&R Block. The money you'll spend (their fee is based on the amount of paperwork you make them do) will be well worth it. A good accountant will make sure you get what's due you. And boy, does it feel good to get those piles of receipts off of your desk and onto someone else's!

When you're done with your federal income taxes, you'll also have to file tax returns for your state and possibly pay even more if you live in a city. That's right: more annoyance. To find out which state forms you'll need, log on to the Federation of Tax Administrators www.taxadmin.org and click on *Links* and then *State Tax Forms*. Usually you can fill out a form by copying lines directly from the federal form, so it's not that much more work, really.

Accountant or no accountant, the key to getting your taxes done in a timely manner is keeping things organized. This means credit-card statements in one folder; cash receipts in another; bills, bank statements, and everything else all neatly labeled. If you ever get audited, you'll need to prove you spent and earned what you actually claimed. It's recommended you keep these receipts and bills in your file box for five years.

I have to give the IRS a little credit. They've made it easier to file, especially now that you can do it online at www.irs.gov. If you actually take the time and read the instructions on the forms themselves, you should be okay. Or, pick up the forms the old fashioned way at the library, local IRS office, or post office.

Once it's all together, read over everything. Make sure you have all of the right forms included in your returns. Check to see that your address and Social Security number are accurate and that you've done your math correctly. If you have to pay, make sure you've made out your check in the correct amount and actually signed the thing! Don't forget to make copies of everything for your files. And don't wait until the last minute! The earlier you file, the earlier you'll get your refund! I know it's so incredibly boring, but it is kind of empowering to do your own taxes.

Money Buzzwords

Even if you don't make enough to save, it's never too early to educate yourself on money and finance. If the only things you do are curb your spending habits, get yourself out of debt, and begin to read up on investment options, you'll be way ahead. Think of *yourself* as a stock. You want to increase in value over time. Use this time to build a foundation and embark on your career. Your own net worth will go up because of what you yourself are becoming—a valuable asset to the work force.

When you're ready, take baby steps to Wall Street. I used to shy away from the whole money and investing thing because it just seemed too overwhelming. Bull markets, bonds, no-load, load—who needed it? I had no clue! So, before we do anything else, let's go over some commonly used market terms. Do whatever you want with these words, but at least be able to understand what they mean so that later you can use them to help you.

Stock An ownership share in a company, which can be purchased by the public.

Bond An instrument used to borrow money, maturing over a set period of time with interest, after which the bondholder can cash in. Remember those lame confirmation gifts you got from Aunt Ethel? Well, guess what? They're not so lame anymore.

Dividend A share of a company's profits paid out (usually in cash) to the stockholder.

Junk bond A high-risk bond with a low credit rating and a higher yield. I include this for no reason other than it sounds cool to throw around at cocktail parties.

Mutual fund A portfolio of individual stocks managed by a professional. Mutual funds offer instant diversification, meaning you get shares of a variety of companies performing at varying levels which balance each other out, making your mutual fund a relatively safe investment. Fees will vary depending on how actively or passively the fund is managed.

Index fund A mutual fund made up of stocks attempting to mirror the performance of a major market index. An example is the S&P 500 Index Fund. This is a group of 500 leading company stocks representing a wide range of industries. Index funds are a common choice for new investors because they offer diversification and low transaction fees. Losses from one stock will theoretically be balanced out by gains from another, keeping risk to the investor relatively low. Basically, an index fund is a relatively safe way to get market returns without following the market too closely. Other index funds include NASDAQ Index funds and Dow Jones Index funds.

Load A commission paid on the purchase of a mutual fund.

No-load (fund) A mutual fund without a commission.

Money market account A liquid account (one in which money can be withdrawn without a penalty) that offers a low interest rate and is generally used for short-term investments.

CD Certificate of deposit. A no-risk, low-return, interest-bearing instrument that pays a fixed interest rate amount over a set period of time. A CD offers a slightly higher return than a money market account.

Capital-gains tax Tax assessed on profits (such as money you make when you sell a stock).

Blue-chip stock A stock issued by a large, well-known company with a general record of solid performance.

Bear market An extended period of falling stock prices when everyone gets depressed and thinks they're broke.

Bull market An extended period of rising stock prices when everyone thinks they're rich and buys things they can't afford.

Dollar cost averaging Investing a set amount of money in a mutual fund on a regular basis. This allows you to buy more shares when prices are lower, but you'll get fewer shares when prices are high, thus averaging your stock price so you don't have to worry about when to buy and sell.

IRA Individual retirement account. A personal, tax deferred retirement account to which an employed person can contribute annually.

Roth IRA Established as part of the Taxpayer Relief Act of 1997, this is a retirement plan that allows taxpayers with certain income limits to contribute a set amount into a tax-free savings account. It's a great thing to set up through a discount brokerage firm if you don't have a full-time job.

401(k) plan A retirement plan similar in nature to an IRA, sponsored by an employer. Pretax contributions are taken directly out of your paycheck as an investment, and many companies will match a portion of what you put in. Plans vary by company.

403(b) plan A retirement plan offered to employees of not-for-profit organizations, similar to a 401(k).

Keogh plan A retirement plan for self-employed people.

Morningstar Inc. A global investment research firm that helps people make educated decisions about their investments (stocks and mutual funds). It's definitely worth your while to learn more about this company. Go to www.morningstar.com for more information.

Starting Your Portfolio

Don't laugh. Yes, you too can have a portfolio. Say it: "portfolio." Sounds cool, doesn't it? Now pretend you're at a cocktail party: "Yes, I'm managing my portfolio," or throw in the name of one of your friends: "Matt Sanders is managing my portfolio."

Okay, now let's figure out what this means.

The key to successful long-term investment strategies is a *diversified* portfolio. You don't want to put everything into one company for obvious reasons (Hmmm. . . can anyone say Enron?). And you'll need to keep some money liquid for different stages of your life, keeping your short-term goals (such as a car or grad school) separate from your long-term goals (such as a beach condo or your future kid's college fund). If you have a full-time job, you should invest in your 401(k) as soon as you're eligible. If you don't, or your company doesn't offer a 401(k), open a Roth IRA as soon as you can.

A good place for beginners to buy an index fund or learn more about Roth IRAs is with a mutual fund family or a discount brokerage firm. Try and steer clear of firms currently under investigation for fraud. You may also want to look into *exchange traded funds* (ETFs), which offer some of the same advantages as mutual funds but are traded more freely, like stocks. To reiterate, index funds are a safe way to start, simply because one stock won't make or break your investment and you won't have to dedicate too much attention to following them. If you're only in it for the short term (less than five years), stick with a money market fund or CD.

Most financial advisors suggest investing in the stock market only if you're planning on staying with it five years or more. Hopefully, in that time, you'll be in a better place to take a little more risk. Since investing is really about assessing your own tolerance for risk and possibly incurring some losses, if you know how much you can afford and how much of a hit you can actually tolerate, you'll feel less freaked out.

If you're really interested in learning more about money and investing, take a Saturday seminar or a continuing education class at your local community college. Here you'll meet lots of people like yourself who want to learn how to be smart about their investments but don't know where to start. The Learning Annex (www.learningannex.com) offers inexpensive classes in New York City, Seattle, San Francisco, Los Angeles, and Chicago.

It's always worth reading more on money matters, especially for women making it on their own. Here are some of my picks for the some of the better resources out there:

Smart Women Finish Rich: 9 Steps to Achieving Financial Security and Funding Your Dreams (Revised Edition) by David Bach, Broadway Books.

A Woman's Guide to Investing by Virginia B. Morris and Kenneth M. Morris, Lightbulb Press.

Money Resources

Budget-Minded Banks

Multi-city Banks

Washington Mutual This bank is really making a name for itself nationally, so I'll single it out. Washington Mutual offers free checking with no fees and no minimum balance, as well as over 2,500 ATMs nationwide. Log on to www.washingtonmutual.com to find a branch near you. 800-788-7000

Wachovia On the East Coast (from Florida up to Connecticut), Wachovia is another bank with new branches opening by the minute. They offer free checking with no fees and no minimum balance. Catch a promotion and you'll get to use other banks' ATMs for free as well. Log on to www.wachovia.com for more information. 800-922-4684 (800-WACHOVIA)

Bank of America With branches in all major cities, sign up for their MyAccess Checking, which gives you free checking with direct deposit and requires no minimum balance. www.bankofamerica. com. 800-900-9000

City-Specific Resources

Boston

Eastern Bank
www.easternbank.com
800-EASTERN (800-327-8376)

Branch locations:
    101 Federal Street
    265 Franklin Street
    246 Border Street
    470 West Broadway
    Shaw's East Boston
    Additional locations outside of the city

Number of ATMs: Over 50 branches outside the city with ATMs.

Basic Checking Account Rules: No minimum balance, no monthly service charges.

Free unlimited check writing, three free ATM transactions monthly at non–Eastern Bank ATMs.

Sovereign Bank
www.sovereignbank.com
877-SOV-BANK (800-768-2265)

Branch Locations: More than 30 in Boston, with more in surrounding areas.

Number of ATMs: Over 42 around Boston.

Basic Checking Account Rules: No monthly service charge, no minimum balance, no per-check charge, unlimited check writing.

Chicago

Mid America Bank Chicago
www.midamericabank.com
708-410-4444

Branch Locations: Over fifteen locations in Chicago. Even more in the surrounding areas.

Number of ATMs: 17 in Chicago, more in outlying areas.

Basic Checking Account Rules: Totally free checking, requires no minimum balance, no per-check charge, no monthly service charge.

North Community Bank
www.northcommunitybank.com
773-244-7000

Branch Locations: Over 15 locations in Chicago metro. More in surrounding areas.

Number of ATMs: Over 80.

Basic Checking Account Rules: The Freedom Account: free checking, $100 minimum to open. Direct deposit or minimum balance required for no fee.

Los Angeles

Wells Fargo Bank
www.wellsfargo.com
800-869-3557

Branch Locations: 10 branches in Los Angeles. More in surrounding areas.

Number of ATMs: Over 25 and some of them talk!

Basic Checking Account Rules: Free checking with direct deposit; otherwise, small monthly fee.

New York City

Amalgamated Bank
www.amalgamatedbank.com

Branch Locations:
    15 Union Square
    1745 Broadway
    301 3rd Avenue
    564 West 125th Street
    52 Broadway

Number of ATMs: Only at branches, so while banking is cheap, this could be inconvenient if one's not near your place.

Basic Checking Account Rules: Free checking with no minimum balance, no monthly maintenance fee, no per check charge.

Independence Community Bank New York
www.icbny.com
800-732-3434

Branch Locations:
    250 Lexington Avenue
    169 7th Avenue
    43 East 8th Street
    864 8th Avenue
    108 Hudson Street
    51 Avenue A
    2275 Broadway
    More in Brooklyn

Number of ATMs: Only a few at branches.

Basic Checking Account Rules: No minimum balance. No fees.

Washington, D.C.

Chevy Chase
www.chevychasebank.com

800-987-BANK

Branch locations: 16 branches in D.C., more in VA.

Number of ATMs: over 800 ATMs in metro area.

No-minimum checking: $5/month with direct deposit, $6/month without
Free direct-deposit checking: Free with at least one direct deposit per statement cycle, no minimum balance.

Sun Trust Bank
www.suntrust.com

800-786-8787

Branch locations:
    1750 New York Ave
    1445 New York Ave
    1900 F Street
    900 17th Street
    1100 G Street
More in MD and VA

Number of ATMs: 5+ in all areas.

Free checking: Free checking with no minimum balance or direct deposit requirements.

Part 2

Working

3

$\sim\sim\sim\sim\sim$

Opening the Door

How to land a job
(or anything else)
with confidence

Someone once gave me some very useful advice. While interviewing me for a job, she asked me to describe the best way to network in five words or less. I couldn't answer, so I sat there looking like a lost sheep. "Turn one person into five," she said sternly. "Oh," I said. I didn't get the job, but I never forgot that rule.

Living in New York City taught me a lot of things, but the biggest thing it taught me was how to deal with people. With so many people concentrated in such a small amount of space, there were always at least ten of them in my face at all times. From the crowds on the subway to the lines at the bank, bagel shop, and grocery store, I quickly learned that in order to make it in a big city, you simply can't avoid dealing with people. So it soon became apparent that I was going to have to master one thing—

Networking

The word alone sounds intimidating. It's also become so clichéd that just hearing it makes you want to run. But, simply put, networking is the smartest way to get *anything* you want in life. It's about being in the know, gathering information, and meeting the people who can help get you where you want to go. Whether it's scoring an inside tip on an apartment, finding a guy you might actually want to date, or securing a job interview, networking is the way to do it. The thing to remember about networking is that it exists everywhere. Andy Warhol once said that everybody is a potential client. Just because someone doesn't look the part doesn't mean she doesn't have the goods. Some of the best contacts are made by simply saying "hello," even if you're on a bus ride in the middle of nowhere. You just need to relax and open your mind to a new conversation. Don't be afraid to *schmooze* a little.

Networking Events

These things used to make me so nervous I wanted to throw up. It felt like a competition to see who could gather the most business cards—all while clutching a cell phone, a martini, and a Kate Spade tote (okay, so I had the *Nate* Spade street version). They come in all forms: cocktail parties, dinner cruises, alumni functions, basketball games, weddings, bar mitzvahs, and even funerals. Still, as frightening as they are, they work. Sometimes you need to fake it and play the game. If you're really dedicated to making networking a part of your life, you might as well try out a few of these things. It's kind of like going to the gym. You may get nothing out of it at all, but at least you can say you went.

Sooner or later, you'll see a few networking muscles develop. The more you do it, the better you'll get.

Once you're at a networking event, here are some useful tips in mind:

- **Don't sprint to the buffet line** Nobody wants to shake your hand while you're balancing a plate of shrimp and cocktail sauce. First of all, it'll seem as if you're more concerned with filling your stomach than meeting people. The buffet line is really a diversion—it's somewhere to go when you're taking a *break* from the crowd. Eat before you go. Grab a stuffed mushroom here, take a piece of brie there, but don't walk around with a heap of tortellini. It's not becoming. Instead, focus your attention on who you want to meet and why. Yeah, I know, it's easy to look busy standing by the food. I used to do this until I realized I wasn't gaining anything except for a few extra pounds. You're allowed to hold a glass of wine. It'll give your hands somewhere to go.

- **Conquer your fear** Take a deep breath and go introduce yourself to at least two new people. Be honest, direct, and as confident as you can without being phony. It's difficult—in fact, really difficult—but try saying something simple like, "Hi, Mr. X, I'm Robin. I really admire your work and was wondering if you had a few minutes to give a novice some advice about your industry." I know it sounds stupid to practice, but it helps if you stand in front of the mirror.

- **Do your homework** Call the sponsoring organization beforehand and find out who's going to be at the event. If you had to register to get in, chances are the attendees will be known ahead of time. Other times, trust your intuition. If you think someone is worth meeting by the way she looks or her general aura, go with it and introduce yourself. If she's not the VP of HBO, then at least you've challenged yourself to make an introduction and, just maybe, you'll meet a new friend. See the list of networking resources at the end of the chapter. Something else to keep in mind: "It's really helpful to know a little about the person with whom you're talking," says Karen McGee, director of career services at Syracuse University's Newhouse School of Communications. Try doing an internet search on the individuals or companies. Find out what their most recent projects were, their latest campaigns, any current news, bios, etc. Give yourself some ammo to bring to the event. It will feed your confidence and make you stand out in a conversation.

- **Read up** It's really important (make that *imperative*) to know as much as you can about the industry you're trying to break into. Trades, daily newspapers, magazines, online sources—the more you know, the better. Try to make reading part of your daily routine, even if it means getting up thirty minutes earlier than usual. You'll feel empowered and have the tools you need to get ahead. A great way to do this without shelling out cash for subscriptions is to plop yourself at the library or your favorite bookstore and read.

- **Act your age** Nobody likes a poser. If you're trying to get into medical school, don't pretend to be a doctor. Be informed and be knowledgeable, but don't try too hard to impress unless you really know your stuff. Better to ask lots of questions than to try to come across as having all the answers. People will see right through you if you don't.

- **Don't ask for a job; ask for advice** Try a little tact here. People love talking about themselves. Use this tool to its fullest extent. Questions like "How did you get your start in the business?" and "Tell me about your background," open the door for a longer conversation. Immediately jumping to "I'm looking for a job" puts someone on guard and makes him think you're only out to get something. Networking is about building long-term personal relationships. You may not get immediate satisfaction, but good questions and timely follow-up will help you immensely in the long run. But don't waste your entire evening in a long-winded conversation with someone you're not really interested in either. If you find someone pontificating too long about the "good ol' days" of college or his particular industry, thank him for his kind assistance, say you don't want to monopolize his time, and move on. Now's a good time for that shrimp.

- **Dress appropriately** Going to a tailgate party? Stay away from the business suit. Of course, if you're going to a networking breakfast, feel free to break it out. Going to a cocktail party? Black works. Try and gauge the event and the industry it's for. That way you won't stick out like a sore thumb or feel ill at ease. Also, wear something you're comfortable in. It's no fun tugging at your skirt for the entire evening or worrying that your new hot pink bra is showing. Don't go nuts spending money on clothes either. Instead, buy one "networking outfit," something sharp, and one "interview outfit," something a little more professional. If you feel good in what you're wearing, you'll have an added sense of confidence. You can get great deals from the shops listed at the end of the chapter. Also, for great deals online, try www.bluefly.com.

- **Be assertive** This is perhaps the most difficult aspect of networking: asserting oneself without being too annoying. Remember, your goal is to get information that will help take you to the next step. This may not mean getting an interview immediately, but it may lead you to the person who will get you there. If you're talking with someone for a while and finding it productive, don't be afraid to ask if you can call her to talk further. Questions like: *Is there someone you know who might be willing to talk with me? What professional organizations are you a member of? Would it be okay for me to give you a call next week?* are good ways to get people to open their Blackberries for you. You should also remember that you, too, are bringing something to the table. "Know what you have to offer," adds Karen. Remember that a good employer is always on the lookout for new talent. If you sound wishy-washy, you won't make a strong impression. Be able to answer the question "What skills do you think are your strongest?" with gusto. Don't just tell someone what you think they want to hear. If you want to be a graphic designer, then say that, even if you're talking to an industry expert. Be as specific as possible. Confidence sells.

- **Learn how to shake hands** Shaking hands is an art. A strong, well-shaken hand leaves a lasting impression. The converse is also true. Shake hands like a limp fish and there go your brownie points. The goal is not to cut off circulation, but to be firm, confident, and secure. Practice with your friends.

- **Always repeat a name** This is one of the quickest ways to build your own list of contacts. Don't overdo this, but as soon as you meet someone, repeat her name. Do it at the end of your conversation, too.

- **Make sure you have the right tools** If you're going to a true networking event, you should bring an updated resumé and a business card that has your name, phone number, and email to leave behind. Keep it simple. You don't have to spend $500 investing in a graphic designer. Look online at places like www.businesscards.com or go to Staples. For around $20, you can design your own. Or use www.vistaprint.com; they offer free business cards if you let them advertise on the back. Another big must: make sure your resumé is accurate and up to date. Don't say you were an executive producer if you were a production assistant. Very bad.

- **Let jerks be jerks** There are plenty of them out there. Some are bullies. Others just don't give a hoot. Recognize that not everybody is out there to help you; most aren't. Every now and then you'll meet a genuinely nice person who'll give you all the time in the world. The people who are in a position to help you are usually very busy. Recognize this. But your time is valuable, too. If you feel someone's jerking you around or trying to lure you into something not right for you, say a polite thank you and continue on your merry way.

- **Pay your dues** Sometimes the only way to get your foot in the door is to intern. You know, work for free, volunteer—call it whatever you want. It doesn't matter how many degrees you have or how old you are. The more competitive the career, the more likely it is you're going to have to put in your time without pay, at least for a while. Suck it up and give 'em your best shot. Ask if there are any volunteer opportunities (even if a company isn't hiring) and then structure your work schedule around it. This will show you're willing to do whatever it takes to get your foot in the door. If you're good, you'll probably get noticed in less than six month's time.

- **Not sucking up** While we're on the subject, let's talk about sucking up for a minute. There's plenty of room for flattery and compliments, just make sure they're genuine. If you lay it on too thick, you'll be viewed as transparent. Kudos are fine when they're deserved. You can say you like the way someone handled a client, or even that you like her haircut, but just don't do it every day. One exec said he was disgusted every time a particular intern came to a meeting because the intern dispensed compliments left and right and had no sense of when to stop.

- **Don't get discouraged If you're not the queen of schmooze** If it were easy, everybody would do it. If you're shy, that's okay. Shy people can have great conversations. Try to get into smaller groups rather than larger ones where you won't feel dominated. A one-on-one conversation utilizing the same tactics will get you just as far. Be brave and keep practicing. Force yourself to go to at least one new event a month. You'll be surprised at how well you'll do after a few of these. Try practicing on new people you meet at a dinner party or on an airplane.

- Follow up You must follow up with every single networking contact. This is just as important as making the contact itself. You should do this within twenty-four hours of meeting someone. If she doesn't immediately return your call, don't give up. If you tell someone you met at a party that you're going to send her a writing sample, do it right away. She might forget about you if you wait too long. Also, short hand-written notes are a great way of saying "It was nice meeting you!" and add a personal touch when you aren't sending anything official. Making the contact is only the beginning, so don't let your hard work go to waste.

- Relax Networking is all about talking to people. Are you a people person? Do you like learning about others? Are you *remotely* interesting? Then you have nothing to worry about! Go in, feel confident and knock 'em dead!

Schmoozing Scenario

Still not sure how this whole thing works? Here's a sample of what could happen to you:

The Set-Up

You just happen to be sitting next to the director of marketing at Miramax films at your friend Rodney's wedding. As soon as you find this out, your knees start shaking. You knew she'd be there, but sitting next to you? And so we arrive at a perfect networking situation. You've wanted to work for Miramax since college but nobody has responded to the hundred-and-one resumés and standard cover letters you've already sent. You tried calling once but you hung up when the receptionist answered for fear of sounding stupid. Well, now's your chance, so don't blow it!

When to Launch into the Conversation

Timing is key. You don't want to look like you're only there to network. This is a social event. You're having fun, remember?

VICTORY!

Marianne M. graduated from Syracuse University at a time when nobody was hiring. Determined to get a job in film development, she researched fellow S.U. alums at the career center and came across the name of a top producer. After reading in the trades that he had recently been promoted to VP of production at a major motion-picture company, Marianne took a risk. She picked up the phone and called his office. Coincidentally, he picked up his own line. She introduced herself and told him simply that she had called to congratulate him on his recent promotion, "from one S.U. alum to another." That's all, nothing more. Impressed with her drive, he asked her what she was up to, as he now needed an assistant. Could she fax over her resumé and references immediately? Several conversations later, without ever meeting Marianne in person, he hired her over the phone. Within seventy-two hours she packed up her stuff from her parents' house in Delaware, moved into a hotel in Los Angeles, and started work the following Monday. Now she's reading scripts, handling appointments, and working her way up the production ladder. All because she took a chance.

You've just returned to the table after a sweaty round of the *hora*, so your adrenaline is pumping. Now's the right time to meet-and-greet. The bandleader has just requested that everyone return to their tables. "The salad is being served," were his exact words. Nothing like a little schmoozing over some radicchio. Introduce yourself. Just do it. Put your hand out and say: "Hi, I'm Emily, it's a pleasure to meet you." She'll most likely return the handshake. If she doesn't, you have a major problem. So now, go ahead and try this:

YOU: I'm really glad Rodney seated us together. I've heard a lot about you.

HER: Really, I don't know squat about you.

Okay, maybe she won't say this, but she'll likely say something to the effect of "Really?" while wondering who the heck you are.

YOU: I've always been a huge fan of Miramax. I hear you just optioned _____.

Here's where your strategy comes into play—you should know something about the company and know which projects were recently acquired. You know this from your weekly reading sessions at the bookstore.

YOU: I read that the writer worked for six months on a farm to get a better sense of how to write from the perspective of a cow.

HER: That's pretty funny. I actually didn't know that.

You've just informed an exec of something she didn't know without doing it in an annoying way. Nice work!

YOU: Have you been with the company a while?

HER: About fifteen years. I started in the mailroom and then worked on up to director of marketing. It's a great place.

The goal now is to get her to ask you what you do. If you're lucky, she'll say something like, "By the way, what do you do?". But more likely, you'll probably sit quietly for a moment and have to launch into it yourself. What the heck. Take a deep breath and keep talking.

YOU: Right now I'm freelancing [*try to use words like* freelancing *or* consulting—*it sounds better than* temping] for a few different places in their marketing departments. I do mostly copywriting and I love it. But I'm always looking around.

You're keeping it real here. You don't want to look like you hate what you do. That'll make you less marketable.

HER: Well, I wish I could say we're hiring right now, but it's not happening. Sounds like you're doing some interesting stuff though."

Don't freak out—it's not over. This simply means she can't offer you a contract right here and now, next to the dinner rolls. Keep the door wide open.

YOU: I'm sure it's tight everywhere now. I actually just finished a project for ___ and I'm working on ___. But, if it's okay, do you mind if I send over some writing samples just in case you need someone for a project?

HER: Sure, why not.

After the Salad

At this point you've gotten up and down a few times to dance. The chicken cordon bleu is being served. Try to loosen the conversation up a bit so you're not only talking about work.

YOU: How long have you known Rodney?

HER: I met him after graduate school in blah, blah, blah.

You don't really care how long she's known Rodney; you're just getting her to open the door for you to throw in some humor and to deepen the personal connection between you. She doesn't need to know this. Now's a perfect time for a personal story.

YOU: Did he ever tell you about the time that his mother caught him with Jeanette in the laundry room?"

You don't have to really dig up something rude here (especially if she's a relative!), just something funny and memorable. I can't help you with this one.

Later that Evening

YOU: It was really great meeting you, NAME. (Always repeat a name.) Oh, before I forget, let me get your address so I can send you those writing samples. I almost forgot!

This is you trying to sound blasé. You've been waiting for this moment since the salad arrived. Just sound like you almost forgot—you'll seem less desperate. Make sure you have a pen tucked away inside your beaded handbag and then grab a cocktail napkin from the bar. Very Hollywood.

HER: "Great meeting you too. Give me a call."

Bingo. You got the info. Now it's up to you to follow up.

And you didn't even want to go to Rodney's wedding.

Jobs Full Speed Ahead!

See, that wasn't so bad. A few weddings, and you'll be a pro! So now, why not take a stab at another very challenging job tactic?

Cold Calls

There's a reason these things are called cold calls. They're icy, they're awkward, and they can really make a girl shiver in her boots. Maybe that's why sales jobs pay such high commissions. Cold calls really suck. But you still gotta make 'em, no matter what industry you're in. And making them is as simple as picking up the phone. Want to know if a particular company's hiring? Pick up the phone and call them. Want to talk to the sales director of a company you think you want to work for? Call her up and ask her for some advice. I'm not saying you'll reach her, but it could happen. Cold calls are part of the game, whether they're done over the phone or literally by walking into someone's office (yes, people have done this too—even though in some industries it's really not appropriate). The key is to keep doing it. Here are some tips to help you get over the fear.

One Word: ASSISTANT

The assistant is just as important as the person you're trying to reach. Knowing this is key to successfully reaching the people with whom you really want to speak. The assistant can be your best friend if you know how to talk to her. And, whether they like to admit it or not, they're gatekeepers—the people who can make your life miserable or blissful, depending on their mood.

Assistants have their own issues with power and sometimes the only way to express it is with people on the phone. Your job is to *empower the assistant*—to make her feel as if she's the important one, because eventually she will be. Treat the assistant like dirt and you won't get anywhere, fast.

I once sent a query letter for a film script directly to the assistant after talking to her for over an hour about my idea. I asked her honestly what she thought and if she'd like to read it. I didn't even mention the name of the producer. I knew the assistant would pass it on if she liked it so I wasn't concerned. When I finally sent a letter to the producer outlining my idea, it was two months later. And guess what? The assistant now was the producer! I was in the office with her for a meeting a week later.

Generally, the assistant is the one who reads everything first. If she doesn't like it, it won't even make it to the next level. So, if you're making a cold call, talk to the assistant for a while. Tell her what you're looking to do and ask for *her* advice. Now, if for some reason you actually get the head cheese on the phone, you'd better be prepared to sell yourself and do it quickly. Your main points should be addressed within the first few seconds of the conversation: *your name, how you got to her, why you're wasting her time.* After you get these points across, you'll get a general idea of how she's going to respond. Most likely, you'll get some sort of an insipid reply—meaning she's probably doing five other things at the same time. Don't let that deter you. Keep your spirits up and ask her if it's okay to send her something in writing outlining your plan. A cold call followed by a note is the best way to keep your name fresh in someone's mind. Finally, always end the conversation with the goal of getting to the next step: Is she willing to meet with you? Can you call her in a few days? Is there something specific you can send? Would she rather receive it via email or snail mail? The key is to do whatever you can to ensure that there *is* a next time.

Writing Strong Letters and Queries

Marcy H. receives over three hundred cover letters a week. As editor at a major publishing house in New York City, she usually tosses 75 percent of them. Same goes for the hundred-fifty queries a week that Marnie J. receives for film script ideas at her agency in Los Angeles. Bottom line: *Most unsolicited letters and queries get thrown away.* It's best to use your personal contacts to get in. Even with a personal connection however, a strong cover letter is imperative. This is not to deter you from sending unsolicited mail, just be prepared not to hear anything if you do. The best way to get your letter on someone's desk is to do the following:

- **Always get a name** You can bet that a "To Whom It May Concern" letter will get tossed first. Why? Because it's just too darn hard for people to figure out where it's supposed to go. The harder you make it for the people in the mailroom (or an assistant who opens the mail), the more likely you'll fall into the black hole. Always get the *name* and *title* of the person whom you're looking to impress. Then address the letter directly to him. Make sure your spelling's correct. If possible, call his assistant and let him know you'll be sending a letter of introduction, even if there's no job posted anywhere.

- **Have a purpose** Nobody wants to scan a letter to figure out why you've written. Even if it's just to introduce yourself and let someone know how much you want to work for the company, make it clear. Cover letters and queries come in all shapes and sizes, with the more creative industries requiring a bit more innovation, but the most effective ones in all categories address the following points:

  1. Introduction
  2. Purpose of your letter
  3. How you can help the company
  4. Timeline of activity
  5. Conclusion

Think of your cover letter or query as a mini–business plan. Here's a sample of a simple but strong letter from someone looking to be a research assistant for a magazine with no current job openings:

Dear _____:

I am a recent graduate of the University of Wisconsin with a degree in English Literature and a minor in French. I am writing to express my sincere interest in Research Assistant opportunities at _____ magazine. As an avid reader of _____ I am especially interested in your *Health and Wellness* section. While working as a reporter for my college newspaper, I learned the value of meticulous research by writing and fact-checking my own pieces as well as those of my peers. I am skilled at mining information from primary sources to support an article and am relentless when seeking just the right experts to offer quotes in a particular area. While I am aware that there are no current openings with your division at this time, I hope you will keep me in mind for the future. Enclosed is a current resumé and clips for your review. In addition, I would be most interested in coming in for an informational interview at your convenience and will follow up with a phone call in several weeks. I certainly appreciate your consideration and look forward to learning more about _____'s research department.

Thank you very much for your time.

Sincerely,

(Sign your name)

Type your name

Polishing Your Interview Techniques

Think about all the people you know who handle themselves well in public: great communicators, charmers, politicians, even people you meet at dinner parties. You can immediately tell when someone's engaging, because they've just "got it." Generally, successful interviewees come across as *genuine, interested,* and *interesting.* This means they've got something unique to add to a conversation; they've got a certain style of presentation and they're good listeners. All three of these qualities make for a good interview. "And," adds Ronit F., a human resources manager in Chicago, "don't forget to do your homework!" This means researching as much as you can about a particular company before you get in their office. Knowing the market and the business is a sure way to impress. Chit-chat is fine, but keep it short. "I don't want to hear about your nephews," says Ronit, "no matter how cute they are." Also, I shouldn't have to mention this, but dress appropriately. If you think your skirt is too short, then it probably is (unless you're applying for a job at Hooters). Keep an upbeat positive attitude and stay interested, no matter how boring the interviewer may be. And don't chew gum or wear too much perfume. You don't want to be remembered as the Chanel floozy.

Also, you should always come equipped with examples of how you handled yourself in previous work situations. For the most part, interviewers are pretty standard. They'll ask you something like, "Can you give me an instance when you dealt with a difficult work situation?" How did you handle it? Think about these types of questions beforehand so you don't get caught off guard. And bring samples of your work in a clean binder. Finally, no matter how hard it may be, you must ask questions! This doesn't include "What's my salary and when do I get a bonus?". Intelligent questions about the company's policies and practice, departmental responsibilities, future developments, etc., will give you a better picture of the position and let the interviewer know you're truly interested. Even if you think you've got it all down pat, don't say "Nope," when asked if you have questions. Always come prepared with a few smart ones and always act interested, even if you're not. While this job might not be the right fit for you, the interviewer may know of something else that is.

Dealing with Strong Personalities

They're out there, all right. And they come in every shape and size. Small, tall, fat, and thin. The quiet intimidators and the outright bullies. Sometimes you just have to listen. An interview is not the time to get confrontational, so don't let your ego get in the way. If you find yourself in an interview situation where you're being intimidated, your best bet is to try to read the person as best you can and give them the answers they want to hear. There's a reason people act like bullies—they're insecure. And insecure people need to be reassured. Make them feel powerful by giving them the right answer. You'll have to be able to gauge this on your own. But you'll also have to make a decision right there whether or not you want to work for this person.

I once worked for a film producer who pretty much made me feel like dirt. She was a true terror and her movies, well, they didn't get too much critical acclaim. So she acted like a tyrant as a way to express her power. After I was able to rationalize this to myself, I was able to separate her tactics from my feeling bad about myself. I learned an incredible amount from her (especially about how *not* to run a business) and eventually left the job. But she always liked me because I was able to feed her what she needed to feel important. It's a tough thing to do, but here's where politics really come into play. The more despotic a person you work for, the more you're going to have to suck it up during the day. Just think of all the great stories you'll have to tell your friends at night!

Interview Follow-Up

Had a great interview but haven't heard from anyone in two weeks? You sent the *typed* thank you note (yes, there is a difference, especially in more traditional jobs); now it's time to get on the horn. Pick up the phone and call. Express your interest in whatever it is you went to interview for and ask what their time frame is for hiring. Don't wait for them to call you. This is another opportunity to be proactive. This is especially true with creative careers. If you're calling to update an agent on your acting career, you should have something new to say each time you call, such as an invitation to a showcase of your work or a recent booking you got on your own.

QUESTION: But how do I know the difference between persistence and annoyance?

ANSWER: Be able to read people. If you're truly calling with new information about yourself or your project, then you're not being annoying; you're just updating them. But if you're just calling to say hello and nothing more, hoping they'll cast you in their next film, then that's a waste of time.

Handling Rejection

How will I ever face the world again? How many more times am I going to have to do this? Maybe I should have gone to law school; Mom was right, this is no life for an educated girl. Let's see, I've probably uttered these phrases, oh, at least a thousand times? It happens to the best of us—getting canned, dogged, dissed, ignored . . . You think you aced the thing and then get a form letter three weeks later. Well, you may not be able to do anything immediately about it, but if it's a job (or a company) that you really, *really* want, you might as well give it one last try. If you're curious to know why you didn't get the job, then pick up the phone and ask. Also, you may want to write a nice note to your interviewer, explaining how you were disappointed that you didn't get the job and hope to be kept on file if the needs of the company should ever change. This is a classy move. You'll be remembered for this and you may just

Remember the Golden Rule of Networking: Turn One Person into Five

If you meet someone you feel can help you move in a particular direction, get five more names from that person and follow up with each one. Whether it's a friend, a business contact or someone you meet at the bank, if you follow up on all leads, you'll eventually wind up with a fat network of resources.

get a call in a few months time. It's also a great way to keep the lines of communication open.

Surviving rejection is also a must for dreamers. Why? *Because the more you dream, the more you'll be rejected.* Take that for what it is and you'll already be one step ahead of the competition.

Now, what can you actually *do* about it? Here are some of the ways I've picked myself up off the floor. Use whichever ones work for you:

- Use rejection as a tool For every rejection letter you get, send out five more queries. For every audition you mutilate, go on five more. Make it a rule. If you let one measly bad day or one fool get you down, how are you possibly going to play in the big leagues? Make a collage out of your rejection letters. I made wallpaper out of mine.

- Work it off Get a rejection letter? Do ten crunches. No, make that twenty. You'll feel just the slightest bit better. See the fitness resources at the end of chapter 7 for where to do this for cheap (or free).

- Cry Rejection sucks, so it's okay to feel sorry for yourself. Cry and kick and scream and say it's not fair. Call someone and whine— but don't call the same person every time. You need to ration the number of people who listen to you complain.

- Surround yourself with people who understand Find a group of people like yourself who are all going through a similar experience. You'll discover there are plenty of others who are dealing with the same ups and downs. Share your war stories with each other and have a few laughs. You'll feel better.

- Eat chocolate This is a must. But then see *Work it off* above.

- Buy yourself a rejection treat Don't spend a lot here—you can make yourself feel better with the smallest little gift. Get yourself a manicure or a new hat. Don't do it all the time either, since you'll be buying something every day (I did, and my clothes didn't fit after eating it all) but every now and then you're allowed. See the inexpensive clothing resources in Chapter 7.

- Get over It The more you wallow, the more time you waste. Remember that rejection is part of the game, so if you want to stay playing, you're going to have to learn to be resilient.

Once You Get the Blasted Job

Hopefully all this networking, cover letter writing, and cold calling will pay off sooner than later. If you get a job, congrats! It's well deserved. I won't spend too much time telling you how to move up the ladder, because by now it should be obvious. Quickly though, the best way to impress your boss is to do the following:

- Get there before her and stay later than her.
- Don't engage in office politics.
- Keep away from negative people (it will rub off).
- Accept the fact that there will be menial tasks associated with your work and do them with a smile (even if it's fake).
- Be friendly toward your fellow coworkers.
- Stay up-to-date with your industry.
- Make suggestions and volunteer for new assignments.
- Every now and then, when you feel like your job sucks beyond belief, take a deep breath and say to yourself: "I'm putting in my time. I'm putting in my time."

Additional Networking Resources and Job Info

Events, job boards and listings, cocktail parties, seminars, films— you name it, these are places where you can find people who know what's going on. Check 'em out. Also, make sure you're accurately listed in your college alumni database so you'll get all the mailings. Don't forget to sign up for regional events, too.

www.womcom.org
The Association for Women in Communications has both student and professional chapters around the country.

www.Womenforhire.com
Lists information on networking events and career fairs.

www.digitaleve.org
Nonprofit organization for women in new media, technology and communications with local chapters in Chicago, Houston, Los Angeles, Philadelphia, and Seattle, just to name a few.

www.witi.com
Women in Technology International hosts networking events all over the globe and offers information to support women working in technology.

www.mediabistro.com
Posts articles, resources, and great discussion boards as well as comprehensive job listings for media industries all across the country.

www.journalismjobs.com
Lists communications jobs (mostly print) around the country.

www.idealist.org
National and international site for jobs, internships, and volunteer opportunities with nonprofits and community organizations.

www.craigslist.org
Again, you can't lose with this site! Jobs galore!

City-Specific Resources

Atlanta

www.ajcjobs.com
The *Alanta Journal-Constitution* has a decent searchable job database.

www.atlpressclub.org
A solid networking group for professionals with extensive journalism and editorial job listings, including internships.

Chicago

www.staffingthecity.com
Temporary positions specific to creative, marketing, and administrative jobs in the Chicago area.

www.npo.net
The site for Chicago nonprofit jobs, where you can also find lots of positions in the communications industry.

www.chicagojobs.org
Provides great links to support groups, job fairs, mentoring programs, and job sites.

Los Angeles

www.hollywooddigest.com
Has a great list serve for screenwriters and filmmakers.

www.ifp.org
Nonprofit service organization supporting independent filmmakers.

www.wif.org
Women in Film hosts networking breakfasts, lectures, and workshops.

New York City

www.winm.org
Women in New Media offers information, resources, and networking events for people in the New York area.

Washington, D.C.

www.dcjobs.com
A wide selection of jobs in the D.C. area.

www.washingtonpost.com
Check out the jobs section of the *Washington Post*, searchable by keyword, county, and industry.

4

~~~~~~~~~~

Following Your
Creative Dream

And paying the rent
while you're waiting
for that big break

A re you a dreamer? Answer these questions:

- Do you sit at work thinking about ways to get out and follow your
  true calling (dancer, writer, actor, architect)?
- Are you comfortable without a steady paycheck?
- Are you able to structure your own day?
- Are you good at setting deadlines and following them?

- Do you always need someone to tell you what to do?

- Are you one to follow the rules?

- Do you take *no* for an answer?

Now, forget every question except the last. Those were meant to get you in the right frame of mind. If you answered "yes" for that question, then sorry, you're not a dreamer. Go back to your desk. For those of you who answered "no" for that question, this chapter is for you. You're a dreamer. You're someone who cannot understand the word *no*. Someone who'll do anything it takes to make your dream happen. This, of course, comes with a price. Dreamers often experience unimaginable lows, waiting for that callback, for the funding, for the editor to call, for the check to arrive, waiting, waiting, waiting. It's inevitable. Failure and waiting are inescapable elements of dreaming.

Choosing the Right Dream Job

What is it that you really love to do and could see yourself being successful at? Think about it. Now think about your personality and how it suits the pursuit of that passion. If you're a recluse and simply can't talk to people no matter how hard you try, you're probably not going to land a job as a publicist, movie producer, or press agent. Maybe you're better suited as a writer. On the other hand, if having no one to talk to all day gives you suicidal thoughts, then a job as a freelance writer isn't the best choice for you, either. You'll need thick skin to make it on Broadway. If you don't have people skills, you probably won't make manager of the year. So, yes, it's important to pursue your passion, but it's also important to be realistic with your own personality and your own limitations with regards to that passion. Some people are more driven than others. Some people take bigger risks than others. Some people have more natural talent than others. Some people are better able to make ends meet without a traditional job than others. Where do you fit in?

Knowing Yourself

One of the most important decisions you're going to have to make involves being honest with yourself. Are you really able to handle rejection on a regular basis? If not, pursuing your dream may be more difficult than you'll ever imagine. Generally, the more creative the career, the more difficult the process. Since there are no rules for pursuing a dream, you'll have to just keep plugging away. Whether it's pitching articles to editors, auditioning for plays, testing new recipes, or trying to land an agent, you have to have tunnel vision. Make sure you get the right kind of side job that allows you to continue to pursue your dream, otherwise you'll just get caught up in the job and forget about what you're really trying to do.

And feel free to think outside of the box, too! Maybe you want to be a writer but need a steady corporate income. A good compromise could be working as a corporate writer. Try not to romanticize your profession. No matter how great somebody else's successful career seems, chances are there was a lot of hard work involved in getting there.

Adding Reality to Your Dream

Just because you're a dreamer doesn't mean you have to live in the clouds. There are plenty of ways to add practicality to your choices and help give yourself a little more of a foundation. Of course, first you have to decide what it is you want to do. Maybe it's opening a café. Maybe it's starting a band. Whatever it is, you must have a goal in mind. Then, prepare for everyone and their mother to tell you why you shouldn't pursue your dream. "It's too expensive!" "It's no life for an educated girl!" "There's too much competition!" "You'll never make it!"

Tell all of these people to take a hike. (For specific replies to annoying relative questions, see chapter 7). Set your sights on what it is you want and write it down. If your dream is to open a teahouse, you're going to need to research the ins and outs of tea. If it's to become an actor, you're going to have to find out about everything from headshots to training programs to monologues. If you want to become a writer, you'd better start writing. This chapter won't tell you how to do that. What it will do, however, is help you find ways to pay the rent, structure your day, and stay focused while you're pursuing that dream of yours.

First things first—$$$. If you don't have this, it'll be mighty hard to compose your concerto.

Paying the Rent

Generally, dreamers require flexibility for their dreams to come true. You may need to keep your days open for auditions, lunch meetings, or classes. You're still going to need a steady cash flow, but you don't necessarily have to be stuck in an office from nine to five. While we all know about the waiter and temp thing, there are plenty of other unique and flexible jobs that offer a solid paycheck, too. Are you a night owl? Do you have trouble waking up in the morning? Best to get a "day job" that lets you sleep in. Just leave some time to schedule your plan of action. The following alternative choices might be just what you need to feel good about yourself while you're on your way.

Doorperson

You won't be able to do this if you're not in a big city, but if you are, here's the scoop: The average doorman makes $25,000 a year and works approximately four eight-hour shifts a week. But wait! During the holidays, most tenants give between $25 and $100 each as cash tips, depending on the building. An apartment building with two hundred apartments will add around $15,000 in cash to your salary. The job is mostly unionized, can be very competitive, and doesn't always get the best rap, but if you're willing to work off hours, you could make a decent living while you're shooting your independent film. Plus, it almost always includes benefits. In New York log on to www.seiu32bj.org for an inside look at the building services unions and additional contact information.

Another option is that of concierge—a higher end doorperson or *information specialist*. This is a bit more professional in nature—some companies will make you take a test or even show a license. You'll need to have stellar customer-relations skills. A good concierge can command fantastic tips and is well sought after. Sound intriguing? Check out the National Concierge Association at www.conciergeassoc.org to learn more.

Dog Walker

Like dogs? Why not take 'em for a walk at $10 a pup? Walk one three times a day and that's $30. Walk ten three times a day and that's $300 a day. Robyn P. started doing this and eventually left her job as a secretary to start her own pet sitting and care business in New York City, walking an average of five dogs a day at $25 a pooch. "You can easily make $1000 a week in this business if you work on your own," she says from her Upper East Side apartment. "It's all about taking a risk and doing something you believe in."

If you want to be like Robyn, you'll need to spend about $300 on bonding and licensing insurance, get your name out there (local newspapers, posting ads on bus stops, and community centers are all good places to start) and really love animals. Robyn suggests working for a company first to learn a bit about the business before going out on your own. Afterwards, you'll probably be able to command as much as $30 for every half-hour walk (if you walk one dog at a time as opposed to a pack of ten). If you specialize in personalized doggy attention (baths, grooming, etc.), the clients will pay you more. For information on how to become a professional pet sitter, contact the National Association of Professional Pet Sitters (www.petsitters.org). This job is more lucrative in big cities where there's no yard for Rover. If you live in Chicago, check out Central Bark (www.centralbarkchicago.com). In New York, try Central Bark West (www.centralbarkwest.com), and in Atlanta, Critter Sitters (www.critter-sitters.com).

Fact Checker

This is one of the best gigs in the publishing biz. Nab a job at a magazine as a fact checker and you're in. A fact checker is someone who's responsible for verifying the factual content of a feature article or news story. Every quote, every statistic, every lush lash mascara price, every spelling on the Swedish do-it-yourself hair removal kit *must* be verified before it is published. You know how some writers make up quotes to sauce up a story (and we're not just talking tabloids anymore)? Well, the fact checker nips that in the bud by making sure the quote is accurate. It's tedious work and one that requires serious attention to detail. You'll be on the phone a lot. But it's important work and one that will truly sharpen your research skills. For around $20 an hour, you'll also get an inside scoop on everything that goes on inside the magazine or newspaper biz. Some publications are a little more flexible than others. Some will even let you work from home. This is also a great way for writers to meet editors. Contact the research department at any magazine or newspaper and inquire about fact-checking opportunities. If they're looking for someone, you'll have to take a quick test to make sure you know the difference between primary and secondary research, as well as information about pop culture, gardening, politics, or whatever the subject of the publication. Once you land the gig, you're pretty much in and can make the rounds to other publications through word of mouth. Companies like Hearst and Condé Nast run a slew of magazines. If you can nab a fact-checking job at one of these places, you'll stay busy.

While there are fact-checking opportunities nationwide, your best bet is in New York City, as that's where most of the large publishing offices are.

Computer Doctor

If you're really skilled with computers, you may want to consider offering your services to help those who are technologically challenged. Generally, the rule is as follows: The more powerful the executive, the more technologically challenged she is. This means that every head honcho out there is basically clueless when it comes to computers. Set up a little Computer Rx business and post signs around town and in the local papers. Make your services easy to understand so as not to confuse the clients. Try this: *Computer Doctor at Your Service. Your body needs a check-up? Your car needs a tune-up? Save yourself angst and money before your system crashes and you lose everything! Reasonable rates for the following services and more: Cleaning up hard drives, high-speed consulting, upgrading memory, fixing any little annoyances, no job too small!* You get the point.

Tutor/Substitute Teacher

Go fish out your old SAT Scores. Did you score anything near a 700 on either section? If so, call up your local Stanley Kaplan (www.kaplan.com), Princeton Review (www.princetonreview.com), or SCORE Prep office (www.scoreprep.com) and sign up to be an SAT and college prep tutor. The hours are extremely flexible; you'll usually work in the afternoon when school gets out or in the evenings. The hourly fee starts at around $15 to $20 dollars if you work for a company, but can skyrocket to over $200 an hour depending on your specialty. On your own you'll probably make a little more cash, but you'll have to find your own clients, too.

For a steadier source of income, you may also want to consider working as a substitute teacher or teaching English as a Second Language (ESL). One writer summed it up nicely:

"Subbing is the best freelance job I've ever had." Why? "You're done by three P.M., it's well-respected on the resumé and will broaden your scope, the money's great (typical pay in the Northeast starts at $80 a day—a little less in the Midwest and on the West Coast) and you can set your own weekly schedule." But don't think it's gonna be a breeze. "Being a substitute teacher does not equal a free and easy work day," says freelance writer John C. "You are expected to follow a thorough lesson plan which the teacher leaves for you and to interact with students regularly, not just sit there." While you won't work in the summer, you can use this time to tutor kids, too. If you opt to be a full-time substitute, you'll be on call all the time but you'll also get medical benefits. For most part-time substitute teaching positions, you'll need at least an associate's degree (a B.A. will get you a little more money), a clean record, and a sealed, official copy of your college transcript. In Chicago, you might also check out After School Matters (www.afterschoolmatters.org). Here, you can teach a course for after school programs on a technical or creative topic.

Sunday School Teacher

You hated going as a kid, but did you ever think you could actually make money doing this? It's an easy way to express your creativity with kids, who, frankly, are sick of school and need some creative means of education. Jody P. moved to Chicago and immediately contacted a few synagogues while she was looking for a full-time job. Because she held a bachelor's degree and had some experience speaking Hebrew, she got a job teaching three afternoons a week. For $35 per hour, at six hours a week, she was able to bring in some quick cash and interview at her own pace without feeling anxious about money. She also tutored some of her students on the weekends for $50 an hour. Contact your local church or synagogue and inquire about religious school teaching opportunities. The best time to do this is late summer.

Personal Assistant

Be prepared to kiss a lot of ass here. But you'll also make heaps of contacts. If you get in with the right person, you can make a load of cash, enjoy some perks of celebritydom, and possibly have time to develop your own interests. Administrative, organizational, and networking skills are a must. Working as a personal assistant is not for everyone. It may allow for some flexibility, but you'll *always* be at the beck and call of your employer (day, night, or right in the middle of something really important). Make sure to ask for references from previous personal assistants so you don't get stuck with a tyrant. A good place to start is by consulting the Public Relations Society of America (www.prsa.org). Just so you know, it's a very competitive field, so use your networking tactics to get in (see chapter 3). There are also professional organizations like New York Celebrity Assistants or Los Angeles Celebrity Assistants that can help you begin. Whatever you do, just don't start wearing sunglasses indoors.

Real-Estate Agent

Real-estate brokers in big cities (both rental and sales) can make a lot of cash, especially when the market's hot. A typical rental broker's fee in cities like New York and San Francisco can run anywhere from 12 to 15 percent of the *annual* lease. Sales fees run the gamut, averaging around 6 percent. In chapter 1, I told you how stupid you are if you pay a broker's fee for a rental—but hey, if you can't beat 'em, join 'em! If you like looking at apartments and houses, if you're aggressive (real estate is another *very* competitive industry), if you're a people person and have a flair for selling, then real estate might be just the spot for you. Look online for "real-estate courses" in your area or contact a few agencies to find out what they require. Some agencies may also pay for your license if you're lucky. And another great perk: you'll have access to hundreds of apartments before anyone else, especially in the most competitive markets.

Personal Trainer

Do you spend a lot of time at the gym? Are you really into it? Then maybe you should think about becoming a personal trainer. First, you'll need to get licensed or have a degree in exercise physiology. With this, you can get a job at a fitness center, as an in-house corporate trainer, or even take on your own clients. The going rate is vast, spanning from $30 to $500 an hour, depending on your experience (and number of cool Spandex outfits). Contact the American Council on Exercise (www.acefitness.org) for information on getting certified. Then, get crunchin'.

Tour Guide

Every city needs good tour guides—or as one guide put it: "A concierge on wheels." If you have a great memory, know your history, and like talking, this job is for you. Prepare to memorize a tremendous amount of facts. Language skills come in handy, too. You're going to deal with lots of different kinds of people and be asked to take a ton of pictures. Being a tour guide is not only a fun way to make money, it's also a great way to make

VICTORY!

Cynthia B. came to New York to make it as an actress. Instead of landing a job at the local café, she decided to take a crash course in real estate. She shelled out $250 for the class at the New York Real Estate Institute (212-967-7508), another $50 for her real-estate license (renewable every two years), and $15 to take the state exam, and got a job at one of the largest apartment brokers in Manhattan. Now a senior rental agent, Cynthia typically works for a few months at a time, averaging ten to fifty hours per week, and then takes a break to work on her acting career. "It keeps my energy up and allows me to focus on what I want, when I want." Last year she worked for ten months and made $70,000 without missing an audition. No clock-ins and no schedules—everything on her time. Most importantly, she doesn't sit around all day waiting for a callback. "It makes getting rejected from an acting job not so bad when you look forward to going to your day job. I can pick and choose what I want to do. And the best part about it is I'm making money and I feel good about myself."

contacts. For actors, you'll get a chance to practice your audition skills. The hours are as flexible as they come and the pay starts at around $12 an hour plus tips in major cities like Chicago, Boston, and New York. If you're really into giving tours, think about museums, theme parks, theaters, and other attractions in your city that may be looking for guides. Here are a few bus companies to get you started:

Boston Duck Tours: 617-723-3825
Chicago Duck Tours: 800-298-1506
Gray Line New York City Tours: 212-445-0848
Starline Tours of Hollywood: 800-959-3131

Personal Shopper

If you like to shop and know your stuff, call up your local department store and inquire about personal shopping opportunities. You'll need to have retail experience and stellar interpersonal skills—this is a real customer-service-oriented position. Higher end stores, like Nordstrom for instance, even require a portfolio, filled with photos of outfits and hot looks you've put together for clients (or your roommate, but don't tell). Once you land a job as a personal shopper, you'll exercise your trendy talent finding everything from articles of clothing to accessories for a variety of folk. It's also another good way to make contacts. While most department stores offer full-time positions (Bloomingdales, Saks Fifth Avenue, Marshall Fields, Nordstrom, and a few others, all have personal shopping departments), hours can be flexible and you may be able to work nights and weekends. Salaries range from $25,000 to over $100,000, depending on experience. Higher end stores work solely on commission.

Charlene G., a personal shopper in Atlanta, recommends spending lots of time in the store getting to know the lines. "This can be an extremely lucrative business if you know fashion," she says. Charlene typically works thirty hours a week, enabling her to pursue a second career as a fashion stylist. "You can do anything you want if you put in your time, get out there, meet people, and network. It's kind of like running your own business." She also notes how important it is to dress well. "You're representing yourself out there, so it's best to look good at all times." A personal shopper's service is usually free, so you don't have to be a hard salesman, just someone who knows and loves trends.

Another type of shopping you may want to try is mystery shopping. Here, a company will hire you to scout out the competition of a product or service (or even test out their own company's customer-service skills), and you'll be paid to report on your findings. You can make some good cash mystery shopping if you hook yourself up with the right company.

Trade-Show Demonstrator

You can make a killing working trade shows, which come in all shapes and sizes. From huge technology expos in major cities to regional shows in small towns, companies are always looking for upbeat, well-spoken presenters or demonstrators to showcase a product. If you're good at memorizing scripts, smiling, and repeating yourself one hundred times a day, you may want to tap into the trade show market. Most every major industry offers trade shows; the biggest and most fun (not to mention the free stuff you'll come away with) are toy fairs, technology shows, boat expos, and food and gift shows. Generally, a trade show will last around four to five days and will require you to know the company's product inside and out so that when the trade show floor opens, you'll be there ready to demonstrate your wares to the throngs of potential buyers stopping by the booth. You'll repeat the same speech until you're blue in the face, be on your feet the entire time, and drop dead on your bed each night from exhaustion. But the pay is ooooh, so good, with lots of travel opportunities. A seasoned trade show demonstrator can easily make between $3,500 to $5,000 in four days, if not more. The bigger the show, the more competitive the sales team, the more money's in it for you. The trick is getting your first trade show.

If you've got spunk and the personality, try calling the corporate headquarters of a bunch of companies for different industries (electronics, motorcycles, toys, etc.) and ask the receptionist how to get in contact with the people who handle the trade shows. Remember, there's a trade show for every industry out there. Because there's no real clearinghouse for these jobs you may have to make a few calls before someone helps you, but the marketing department is a good place to start. An Internet search in your industry of choice will give you a list of vendors you probably never knew existed. Call as many as you can and then follow up with a professional cover letter and headshot (if you have one) along with a current resumé.

Clown/Party Character

This is a great side job for actors. Look in the telephone book or on the web under "Children's Parties." Many companies who organize these events hire freelance clowns, Nemos, Elmos, Cinderellas, or any other popular character to spend an hour or two entertaining kids at birthday parties. It'll test your improvisational skills, and it's a lot of fun. Of course, it helps if you like kids. The pay ranges from $30 to $50 an hour plus tips. Christmas time is also a great time to contact party planning agencies for company holiday parties.

Catering

There's nothing like a free gourmet meal. You're sure to get this when you work for a caterer (although you may have to sneak under the table to eat it). The work is tiring and the hours are long, but the time will pass quickly. Kitchen staff makes an average of $8 to $12 an hour, while servers can get upwards of $15 to $40 an hour plus tips. From Bar Mitzvahs to weddings to company picnics, there's plenty of work to go around. Contact caterers in your area and inquire about temporary work. Make sure to say you've done this before, even if you haven't. It's a little secret that worked for me.

Flight Attendant

This may not be the most flexible job in town, but it sure gets you where you want to go. Stick with the flight attendant biz for a while and you'll work your way up the seniority ladder to where you can pick your flights. The average pay for a flight attendant isn't fabulous—it starts at around $15,000 a year—but you may also get expenses and per diems, depending on the airline. Most flight attendants work an average of seventy-five hours per month, so you can still have some time for yourself. Says seasoned flight attendant Kiki W., "So many airline personnel begin second businesses simply due to the amount of time off, so it's a great way to supplement another career." Kiki's been flying for American Airlines for almost twenty years and still loves the job.

Some things to keep in mind: You must have good vision, be at least nineteen years old, fit the height and width requirements (they don't measure weight anymore) and have a U.S. passport. The more flexible you are in terms of living, the better. One writer found working as a flight attendant was the best way to work on her travel book—without paying a dime for the travel.

Club Promoter

This is a job for very social types. As a promoter, your job will be to create a buzz about a particular bar or club and attract hot, hip people to the venue. You'll get a percentage of the cover charge for the evening, so the more people that show up to the bar or club, the more money in your pocket. Most promoters work by sending emails, passing out flyers, networking with friends, and talking to DJs and club owners. For a list of clubs and nightlife in most cities in addition to occasional job postings, check out www.joonbug.com. In New York City, try www.impulsenyc.com.

Housekeeper

Some hate cleaning. Others find it therapeutic. If you fit into the second group, consider working as a part-time housekeeper. It's not glamorous, I know, but you can work on your own time, listen to your own music, and make some easy cash. Maybe you specialize in home offices, maybe you only do studio apartments. Get yourself a gimmick and post a few signs around town, on bus stops, or place an ad in the local paper and send emails to your friends at work. You can easily make $100 a day cleaning two apartments, and even more for offices. Again, you gotta like to clean, but if you do, why not make some money while you're at it?

Odd Jobs

To take the housekeeper thing one step further, are you handy? Maybe you know how to set up DSL like no other. Or you know how to split a cable wire and run it through an entire apartment. Perhaps you know how to hang curtains, build shelves, or lay carpet. Whatever your skill, market it. This is something you can do on your own time. Post a few signs around town and put an ad in the local paper. A good handywoman is hard to find. You can charge per hour or per project—your pick. Do a little research to find out the going rate in your area.

Videographer

Are you in film school? Do you have access to a digital camera? If so, why not market your skills as a party videographer? You'll need to be somewhat business savvy for this, and you'll probably need to know about editing, too—most clients want a finished product. But hey, if you're in film school, you probably know how to do it anyway. A skilled wedding videographer can make anywhere from $2,500 to $5,000 an event, depending on the coverage necessary.

These are just a few options to help you. If you're really going to pursue that Broadway career, you're going to need to carve out time to do it. If you can't handle being a waiter, find something else. That way you can call yourself a *consultant*. It will make you feel better when people ask you what you do. The most important thing is to stay positive, no matter what you're doing. Making money is a great way to do this. But remember, you're going to have to work hard to make it happen.

Tips for Managing Your Time

One big obstacle that keeps people from pursuing their dream is time management. That's because managing your time efficiently when you're a dreamer requires a lot of dedication. This holds true whether you've got all the time in the world to follow your dream or you're working a full-time job and pursuing it on the side. Some people may even find it harder if they have all the time in the world, because then they have to structure their entire day around, well, nothing! Organization is key. Whatever situation you find yourself in, you'll need to do the following:

- Set deadlines and goals This will force you to stick to a schedule. Your monthly calendar should include practicing your craft at least three times a week for starters. If you have to wake up at five A.M. to draw your designs, then do it. Make it a Monday, Wednesday, Friday ritual. It's really easy to blow this off. But if you have a goal written on a calendar, you'll be more likely to stick to it. It's also helpful to tell people about your goals and ask them to remind you when the time comes to show them your progress.

- Allot a certain time of day to your dream every day Knowing you have from 6:00 A.M. to 8:30 A.M. to write will help you stay focused. It may be difficult setting your alarm an hour or two early, but if you have to be at work by nine, you're going to need to carve out your own "dream time." In your head, your dream planning should be just as important as the job you're getting paid to do.

- Take a break Don't get too frustrated if you're not meeting your preset deadlines. Take a look at your schedule. Have you tried to cram too much into a month? You won't be productive if you're not honest with yourself. Better to take longer than rush and get something done poorly.

- Don't let your relatives get you down Everyone wants their parents to be proud of them. But unfortunately, not everyone's relatives are supportive when informed their beloved "A" student wants to move to Hollywood to break into acting. You'll get a better response from your family if you have a plan laid out (i.e., how you're gonna pay your rent without begging them for cash)—but you should still be prepared for some resistance. After all, they've invested a lot in you—why aren't you going to law school? Stay focused, positive, and practical, and they'll eventually get it. See chapter 7 for specific answers to their questions.

- Stay fit Staying fit will help you adhere to your schedule. Feeling good about yourself and your body will allow you to release energy so you can stay focused. You don't have to spend a bundle at an expensive gym either (see the fitness listings in chapter 7).

Health Insurance

If you're out there making it on your own and take any combination of alternative jobs to pay the rent (such as the ones mentioned above), chances are you're sporting for your own health insurance. This mean's you're going to have to research the best plan for the least amount of cash. One plus for those who are self employed: you may be able to deduct 100 percent of your health insurance on your tax returns.

Here are a few choices to consider when starting your research:

- Ehealth Insurance Log onto www.ehealthinsurance.com for a comprehensive listing of different plans around the country and get a free online quote.

- Catastrophic insurance Ask your health care provider if they offer catastrophic insurance plans. These can range anywhere from hospital coverage only to more comprehensive services and will likely come with a much higher deductible. While you won't pay a huge monthly fee, you'll get charged more if something happens to you. Use this as an absolute last resort rather than going without any health insurance at all.

- Membership organizations If you're a member of a union such as the Writers Guild (www.wga.org), the Screen Actor's Guild (www.sag.org), the Authors Guild (www.authorsguild.org), or any other for that matter, you may also qualify for their health insurance plan. If you're self-employed, contact the National Association for the Self

Employed (www.nase.org) and see what's available to you. For those living and working in New York City, check out the Freelancer's Union at www.workingtoday.org. Here, you'll find lots of information about health insurance policies for those on their own, as long as you're working an average of twenty hours per week.

Terms You Should Know Before You Shop Around

These terms will come in handy when you start shopping around. Best to get acquainted with them now.

- Deductible The amount you will pay out of pocket each time you visit a doctor or go to the emergency room. The higher the deductible, the lower the monthly fee. If you're someone who gets sick a lot, think about this when asking your provider for options.

- Premium The monthly fee you will pay for service.

- Cap The highest amount you'll have to pay for any one year of coverage.

- Pre-existing conditions Any illness you had before you signed on with an insurance company.

- Network A group of doctors who participate in a particular health plan.

VICTORY!

Cameron S. of Boston, Massachuchetts, had just given birth to her first baby when she realized her dream of being an aerobics instructor wasn't going to be so easy. Not satisfied with staying at home all day and unable to afford daycare, Cameron took her baby and started an aerobics class for new moms. The catch? They had to bring their babies to class, stroller and all. A stroller pushed back and forth up a small hill not only rocked the baby to sleep, but offered a low impact workout for moms wishing to shed some of their pregnancy weight. Six reps of lifting baby up and down created a sea of giggles from the tots and also toned their moms' biceps. Cameron used her noodle to make great money from a unique business. And although she can afford it, she doesn't need daycare anymore.

- Out-of-network Doctors who don't participate in a particular health-care plan. Note: just because a doctor is out-of-network doesn't mean you can't see her. You just may have to pay more to do so.

Types of Health-Care Plans

With so many plans available to the consumer, here's a breakdown of some of the most common:

- Fee-for-Service This is where you pay a percentage and the health insurance company pays a percentage. Generally, these plans allow you to go to any doctor, but you'll also have to file your own claims.

- HMO Health Maintenance Organization. Here, there's no deductible and a small co-pay, but you will also have to see a primary care physician each time you get sick.

- PPO Preferred Provider Organization. You won't necessarily have to see a primary care physician before you see a specialist, and you will also be able to choose your own doctors as opposed to the ones on the HMO's list, but you'll likely incur a higher premium.

- Cobra (Consolidated Omnibus Budget Reconciliation Act of 1985) Extends a company's health coverage plan to former employees and their families for a set period of time after their employment has been terminated. The former employee is responsible for paying a monthly fee for continued coverage, which, by the way, can be costly.

Questions to Ask Your Provider

Once you do get someone from a health-insurance company on the phone, here are some questions you should ask:

- What plans do you offer for individuals?

- What services are offered under each plan? Make sure to ask if your plan covers specialists. If you're planning to visit the dermatologist monthly, you want to make sure it's not going to cost you extra. Also make sure to ask about preventive health care, birth control, and immunizations.

- Is there a cap (limit) on fees in a *Fee-for-Service plan?* If you choose this type of plan, which doesn't have a deductible, make sure you ask this question.

- Do you offer a *noncancelable policy?* This means the provider will continue to cover you as long as you pay the monthly premium.

- Does your policy cover *pre-existing conditions?* Spend some time asking the agent to explain everything in detail, even if you have to ask the same questions over and over. This stuff is really confusing, but you want to make sure you understand your policy.

Final Thoughts on Being a Dreamer

This world is filled with competitive and talented individuals. Be relentless about your goals and you'll eventually make it. You may not make it in the way you had originally anticipated, but something will happen. Really.

5

Entrepreneurs Take a Back Seat to Nobody

Do you have what it takes to start a business?

Your friends all tell you your orange crumb muffins are to die for. People come from miles around to taste your key lime pie. And even though you're sending out resumes to finance companies, secretly, you're wishing you could open a bakery. We talked a lot about dreaming in chapter 4, but opening a business is a lot different than pursuing other dreams. Unlike writing or other trades which can be practiced from home, an entrepreneur needs to have a space (and insurance, and a license, and employees) to fulfill her dream. And this translates into money. So if you've always wanted to open a business or you're unemployed and getting frustrated with the dearth of jobs in your line of work, maybe it's time to really think about what it means to become an entrepreneur.

Is Entrepreneurship for You?

Entrepreneurship isn't for everyone. Owning a business and not having to answer to higher-ups may sound glamorous, but success doesn't come without a price. Some aren't sure if it's always worth it. "I'm married to my job," says Candice R., a small gift shop owner in New Jersey. "I eat, sleep, and breathe the business. Sometimes it's just not worth the anxiety." Be prepared to spend most of your time working. You'll have to serve as your own secretary, mail clerk, and press agent right away, so you should be comfortable wearing a lot of hats. You may also want to think about the city in which you live and how conducive it is to being an entrepreneur. For instance, the rent on a retail space (as well as your living space) in New York City is going to be much higher than in, say, Denver or Atlanta. So if your business can thrive in a less expensive city, you may want to consider a move so your day-to-day expenses are less.

Business Basics

Here are some questions to ask yourself before you even think about starting your own business:

- Are you able to structure your own workday, or do you need someone telling you what to do?
- Can you handle (both physically and mentally) the uncertainty of not always getting a paycheck every month?

- Do you have a business plan?

- Are you comfortable working alone?

- Can you handle working 24/7 for the first five years, maybe more, with no vacations?

- Have you checked out the competition for your business?

- Do you have a realistic picture of how you're going to execute your business?

- Do you know how to market your business?

- Do you have money put away to help get your business off the ground?

The Business Plan

A business plan is useful no matter what you want to do. And it's something you'll want to start working on immediately, as it'll help you flush out your ideas better. Basically, it's a guideline that details your plan of action and shows you know what you're talking about. If you'll be seeking funding, you'll need one of these, no matter how small your business. It will also help you stay organized and be more realistic about your goals. Though it may differ according to industry, a business plan will usually include the following components:

I. Introduction This is the first section someone will read, so you need to make it eye-grabbing. If you're looking for funding to open a restaurant, your first few sentences should explain to the reader why your restaurant is going to be the best one in the neighborhood (and not just because your parents'll eat there!). Note: if you aren't a writer, then hire a professional to help you write a business plan. It's worth every penny.

II. Your plan of action Here's where you write the nitty-gritty details of what, exactly, it is you'll be doing and how, exactly, you'll be doing it. Who will your business target? Where will it be located? What's your unique product? How will it be used in the market?

Writing this section will force you to think realistically about your goals in terms of execution.

III. Market analysis This is where you show that you've done your homework. You'll need to study your market to find out what's already out there. Are there comparable businesses where you're looking to open up? Remember, investors will look for any possible reason to say "no" to your project. The biggest reason for a rejection is usually because it's already been done. Be prepared. Defend yourself against being turned down by knowing what the obstacles are and how you'll overcome them. List the comparable products or services in your area. Then briefly write a sentence or two about why your idea is different.

IV. Marketing and promotion Do you have contacts at the *Today* show? Can you get yourself in the local paper? Anything you can do to help sell your product or service using the media is important to include in your business plan. Publicity sells. It's up to you to figure out how you're going to publicize your biz. Don't wait for your customers to find you. Figure out what strategy works best for you: Direct mail? Paid advertising in local media outlets? Flyers on cars? Screaming on the street corner? There are plenty of ways to be creative without contacts.

V. Timeline for your business Investors will need to see that you've got a plan of action. "I want to open a dance studio one day" is not a plan of action. A month-by-month calendar of your plans (even if they never come to fruition) is. You must demonstrate that you're truly embarking on the process if you want people to believe in you. Scouting out locations, realtors, monthly expenses, projected opening dates, costs, revenue, and profit, etc., should all go into your timeline. Depending on the nature of your dream, you may or may not need something more formal in terms of a spreadsheet. This is where your Microsoft Excel tutorial will come in handy. Leave absolutely nothing to the imagination. In fact, try and think of every possible question someone may have about your plan—especially if you're asking for money upfront. The more you can answer these questions before they're asked, the better position you'll be in.

VI. Sample of your work Whether it's designs for curtains, a portfolio of your best photography, or a plate of those crumb muffins, anyone giving you money will ask to see what you've done. Make sure it's the best representation of you.

VII. About you This is where you make yourself look pretty—very pretty. On paper that is. Write a bio about yourself, what you've accomplished, where you've been. The more you can include about your accomplishments, the better. But be honest. If you weren't the president of your sorority, don't say so. It'll come back to haunt you.

VIII. Summary Here's your final chance to sell it. Combine everything you've just outlined into a few neatly written paragraphs. This is your closing argument.

For additional help writing a business plan, check out the following:

Business Plans Kit for Dummies (with CD-ROM), by Steven D. Peterson and Peter E. Jaret, For Dummies.

Streetwise Complete Business Plan: Writing a Business Plan Has Never Been Easier! by Bob Adams, Adams Media Corp.

Registering Your Business

Are you embarking on this challenge alone, or do you have a partner? Different types of business arrangements require different forms and legal documents. You'll probably fit into one of the categories below:

TYPE	DEFINITION	PLUSSES	MINUSES	TAX FORMS
Sole Proprietor	For those truly on their own. You'll be the only one responsible for all aspects of your business.	Easy to set up. You simply need to register your name and get started.	Yep, you are the one solely liable for all aspects of your business.	1. Form 1040—Individual Tax Return. 2. Schedule C or SE—Self-Employment and Profit or Loss Tax.
Partnership	An agreement between two or more people. Should include a breakdown of ownership, division of profit, intended length of partnership, compensation, and procedures to follow should the partnership be dissolved.	You aren't the only one responsible for keeping the business thriving. And, you don't have to divvy up the profits to outside investors.	Can get sticky if you don't have an attorney draft a legal agreement. Don't leave anything up to chance, or a good friendship can go sour. Each partner can be liable for the other partner's action done in the name of the partnership.	1. Form 1065— (Partnership Income) and/or 1065 K1. 2. Schedule SE—Self-Employment. 3. Tax Form 1040—Individual Tax Return. 4. Schedule E—Supplemental Income or Loss.
Corporation C Corp	Decisions about the company are made by the largest shareholder or the board of directors.	Can raise money by selling shares of the company.	Can be costly to set up and maintain. Records must be kept on everything, and oftentimes the president of the company must answer to the board of directors or stockholders. A lawyer is highly recommended to help set this up. Form 1120—Corporate Income Tax Return.	1. Form 1120—W Estimated Corporate Tax. 2. Form 4562—Depreciation Payroll Tax, Sales Tax, etc.
Corporation S Corp	Same as C Corp. This is more popular than the C Corp. The main difference is that with the S Corp, profits and losses are reflected on your own 1040 returns as opposed to on the corporation's.	Same as C Corp. Profits from S corporation are passed through to shareholders based on their shares owned. Losses are passed through to shareholders based on their shares owned, but only to their capital investment and personal loans made to the corporation. No corporate income taxes are due on S Corps.	Same as C Corp.	1. Form 1120—S Corporate Income Tax Return 1120 S K1. 2. Form 4562 Depreciation, Payroll Taxes, Sales Tax, etc.
Limited Liability Corporation, PC (Professional Corporation) also known as an LLC	This is becoming a very popular arrangement for small businesses, as it combines the elements of a corporation with the tax benefits and relative ease of use of a partnership.	Flexible and less formal than a traditional corporation.	Can get expensive and there's more paperwork to fill out to get started.	Legally, a single person can form an LLC. If you have a partner, you'll need the same forms as a partnership. All income and Social Security taxes are paid on partners' tax returns, form 1040, 1040SE.

VICTORY!

Helga W., of Greenbelt, Maryland, felt the heat immediately after 9-11, when she was laid off from her job as vice president of a top communications firm in Washington, D.C. Instead of sending out a horde of unsolicited resumés and cold calling potential employers, Helga took a strong look at the market and decided to challenge her industry. "I realized the PR world was affected greatly. Clients were no longer going to spend big budgets on their accounts," she says from her newly created home office. Along with a few colleagues from her firm who'd also been let go, Helga formed Missionworks, a public relations firm specializing in not-for-profit and corporate public interest accounts. Immediately they shaved money off the top by each agreeing to work from home. "This allowed us to pass the savings on to the clients, giving us an ability to stay on top of the competition," she says. Helga admits it took a while to get used to the change of lifestyle. She cut back on high rent and commuting fees by moving from the city into the suburbs. But being away from the action was a challenge and forced her to read more in order to stay up-to-date with current trends. Since opening its doors in January of 2002, Helga's client list at Missionworks has grown at a slow but steady pace. Helga's advice to women embarking on their own businesses is short and simple: "Start off with a six-month reserve so you don't starve, work hard, and recognize that you probably won't turn a profit for at least two years. Always charge an upfront fee, no matter how small. And learn how to write a business plan—or pay someone to write one for you."

Not all businesses require licenses (for instance, you don't need a catering license in the state of North Carolina), but you'll need to find out what licenses and forms your state requires. Look under the City Business License Office in the phone book. Also, the Small Business Assistance Center (www.sbacnetwork.org) provides free counseling, seminars, and financial referrals for small business owners. If you want to incorporate, check out a company called My Corporation (www.mycorporation.com). You'll pay for the service, but you'll save a lot of paperwork and headache.

Taxes

If you're sloppy with your checkbook, you'd better whip yourself into shape fast. You won't be able to get away with this with your business. Whether it's monthly projected earnings you'll be reporting or sending in timely sales tax, you'll have to be more organized than ever before so the IRS doesn't come a-knockin'. Hiring a part-time accountant will help ease the stress of doing it right the first time. Before you sell one muffin, you'll have to have all of your documents in place. These include an *Employment Identification Number* from the federal government as well as *State Tax Information*. The Federal Department of Revenue is the place to apply for these documents (www.irs.gov). Click on "Businesses" and then "Small Business" for a list of what you'll need. The IRS also offers free virtual workshops where you can learn about everything from payroll taxes to electronic filing. Remember: you'll need to file both federal and state taxes. Also, see chapter 2 for more information on doing your own taxes.

Trademarks, Patents, and Copyrights

A *trademark* or *service mark* is a word or symbol associated with a particular entity. The trademark will serve to identify your product or service and will be used to market that business. A business name is something that would be trademarked, in addition to a tag line, such as *Just Do It*. If you have a catchy name for your business, you'll likely want to register it with the Trademark Office, so that once you start marketing your product, you'll be protected for a period of ten years. To clear up a common confusion: anyone can use the ™ sign as a way of claiming rights to a particular mark, regardless of whether that mark is filed with the United States Patent and Trademark Office. The ® sign can only be used, however, *after* the USPTO grants a trademark in connection with a particular good or service. It offers more legal protection than a ™. Be prepared to shell out a few hundred dollars for your mark. Also, applying for a trademark takes several months time, so keep this in mind when working on your business plan and marketing campaign.

A *patent* is a legal document issued to an inventor by the U.S. Patent and Trademark Office for a period of time (usually twenty years). A patent protects the inventor by excluding others from making or selling the same invention during that time. This one will cost you the most, as you'll probably want to consult an attorney. On your own, you'll incur filing fees upwards of $700. For more information on patents and trademarks, or to file for either electronically, log on to the United States Patent and Trademark Office (www.uspto.gov).

A *copyright* is used to protect intellectual property, such as a book, music, or screenplay. The work must be completed before you can copyright it. A copyright is relatively easy and inexpensive to obtain. You can do this by submitting a copy of the finished work along with payment and information to the United States Copyright Office. To do this electronically, log on to www.copyright.gov.

Financing Your Business: Grants and Loans

Free Money

Financing your business is the most difficult piece of the pie. Before you think about loans, I suggest doing a little research to see if you can get some free money in the form of a grant. There are plenty of organizations out there looking to give away their money to good businesses—particularly not-for-profit and minority-owned businesses. The best place to start your research is at the Foundation Center (www.fdncenter.org). Foundation libraries can be found in major cities, such as New York, Atlanta, San Francisco, and Washington, D.C. Here, you can spend hours (or days) sifting through binders of material on grant-bestowing organizations. You can also sign up for seminars to help you narrow down your search. The process is worthwhile, even if you're not even thinking about a grant right now. The librarians are chock full of information, so bring a bag lunch and spend the day asking a lot of questions. If you can't get to a foundation library, you can also log on to www.sba.gov (make sure you check out the area specifically targeting women-owned businesses) and click on "Grant Resources" in the "Financing Your Business" section.

Others do much better by asking friends and family to share their wealth. Some ask; some beg. It all depends on how comfortable you are doing this and how much you need the cash. You'll have to decide what works for you.

Loans

If you come up dry from the free money sources, you'll probably have to consider a small business loan. A potential lender will want to know that you are serious about your business. This means you need to be organized and have all of your paperwork in order when you apply for your loan. The business plan will come in handy. Chances are, you'll be asking about a *short-term loan*, which will need to be paid back within a relatively short period of time (usually within a year). One word of caution: Be sure your personal financial situation is in good standing. Do you have good credit? Do you have any collateral (something tangible that can serve as a backup) for your loan? Many times, a lender will look at this first, even if your business plan is perfectly crafted. Why? Because even a perfectly crafted business can fail. If you're a homeowner, you may be in a better position to get a loan than a renter, but each lending institution differs, so make sure to compare your options carefully.

The Small Business Administration offers loan programs, so check their website for detailed information on how to apply. You may also qualify for a nonprofit loan or a physical disaster business loan, depending on the nature of your business and where you're located.

There are lots of different loan options available to you if you do the research. You can find loads of information at the

Office of Women's Business Ownership (www.onlinewbc.gov) for resources in your area.

Business Insurance

A good business insurance policy can mean the difference between your company's success and failure. Hopefully, you'll never have to use it. Too many small business start-ups overlook this essential piece, thinking, "Oh, it's just myself and a partner, what could go wrong?" Well, anything. The last thing you need is a lawsuit on your shoulders should someone decide they were wronged by your enterprise. If you're serving food, it's absolutely imperative that you get insurance, in case someone gets sick from your lemon meringue. If you'll be using your car to deliver your goods (or hiring delivery people), you'll need to get extra coverage for that, too. In addition to *general liability coverage*, which serves as the starting point for most business insurance policies, you'll add on extras depending on the nature of your business. Shop around for the best policy out there. This is time consuming, especially since you'll be considered "high risk" if you've never worked in your line of business before. Take a look at www.netquote.com to get started.

Creative Ways of Finding Space

Finding the right space to set up shop can be incredibly frustrating to a small business owner. Karen W. was all set to open her food delivery business out of her apartment in Atlanta. When she went to apply for her business license, she was all but laughed out of the office because her company wasn't located in a commercial catering kitchen. The health inspector wouldn't even consider her business until this was done. Lesson here? Be sure to know your business and its limitations. Obviously, a food-related business will require more scrutiny, but you can be creative here, too. Some of the best resources may be right in your own neighborhood. Churches, synagogues, community centers, and nonprofit organizations are all good choices if you're thinking of opening a catering business or the like. Many have certified commercial kitchens and only use them for dinners and an occasional meeting here and there. You'll save a load of cash by renting from them. You can probably work out a deal with the organization that benefits you both. Your local Chamber of Commerce, Visitor and Convention Center's Bureau, or City Council Office can help you get started. You'll also need to contact your state's Planning and Zoning office to make sure you're permitted to operate your business from the location you choose.

Charging a Fair Price

After assessing the marketplace, you'll need to come up with a fair price to charge your customers. Think about what others charge for the same product or service. How different is your product from the competition? How much more will someone pay for it (keeping taxes, salaries, any extra fees into consideration)? Obviously, the idea is to turn a profit. So when you set a price, you want to base this on what you'll net. The net is money you get after all the expenses are taken out. A good way to remember this is to think of money falling through an actual net. What's left in the net is what you keep! Also, remember you're going to spend a lot more in the beginning for start-up costs.

Hiring Employees

Many successful businesspeople say that the hardest thing about running their own business isn't the fierce competition or the market: it's hiring and maintaining good employees. The more thorough you are in your search (and the more you can learn about human resources practice), the better you'll be in the end. I highly recommend consulting a professional in this area before you embark on this process.

You'll have to decide if you're going to place newspaper or online ads or use an agency. The best way to find good people is to network. Try and be as specific as possible with what you're looking for and the skills required for your business. Write down a job description for yourself—it'll help you stay focused in the interview process. And be sure to get at least three references from all potential employees so you can make sure you're getting good people.

When you do get someone in for an interview, don't be afraid to ask specific questions, tailored to the job. Questions about how individuals handled themselves in a particular situation will help you assess how they'll handle themselves in your business.

If you plan on having your employees work full-time, you'll need to offer some form of benefits compensation and deal with payroll tax. This can be overwhelming to first-time small business owners, but it's something you should think about for the future. You'll also need to pay employment taxes. Make sure to read up on employee compensation on the IRS website.

Something else to remember as a general rule: If you're good to your employees, they'll be good to you. Creating a pleasant work environment and listening to the needs of your workers (without being a pushover) will pay off in the long term. If you've never managed people before, this can be a real challenge. The more people you hire, the more personalities you'll encounter. A good suggestion is to sign up for a seminar on small business management offered by a human resources specialist. You'll learn a lot about yourself as well as your own management style.

Marketing, Marketing, Marketing

No matter how great you imagine your business will be, if you don't know how to market it, you might as well not open. Some of the most absurd ideas are huge successes, while brilliant ones are left in the dust. Why? Marketing. Some argue that marketing is more important than the product itself, and I tend to agree.

This can be a daunting process if you aren't organized. Successful marketing involves knowing your business inside-out as well as understanding the demographics you're targeting. To keep yourself from getting overwhelmed, keep a file of marketing ideas as soon as you begin thinking about your business itself. Spend half your day working on your business and the other half thinking about marketing it. Marketing can get very costly, so you'll need to have an idea of what you're willing to spend.

Branding

This is a process that associates a name, tag line, or image with a particular product or service. Advertising execs throw this term around left and right. The idea is to take your business, assign a name and/or logo to it, and get the word out like mad. You want the name and logo to be consistent with everything that's connected with your business. From letterhead to delivery bags, books to a line of dolls, a consistent look and feel to your business's name and design will help brand it in the marketplace. Some ways to help you brand your business include the following:

- Create a web presence When thinking of domain names, try to use something that will be easy for people to remember if they're doing a search online. Everyone gobbled up the .coms in the late '90s, but now there's plenty of different choices to go around, even if it's a .net, .tv, or .info. In terms of your name, getting too abstract will make it difficult for people to find your product or service (unless you're a marketing goddess and can brand the heck out of some random title that doesn't mean anything). Again, be realistic about how you're going to market your product so you don't wind up with a half-baked campaign. Once you have a name in mind, log on to www.register.com to check if your domain name has been taken. When you find one that's available, you can buy it for about $30 a year. Hire a designer or design student (or do it yourself) to put together a site for you. One page may be all you need, depending on your business. If you're selling your product online, it will cost more to have a secure shopping cart system set up. No matter what you're doing, people will check you out online, so you really need some sort of presence. Then you'll want to make sure you get top visibility. You can do this by submitting your website to search engines such as Google and Yahoo (for a fee), but you may not necessarily be the first page pulled up when people do a search for a product or service. Web marketing is a whole world of its own and warrants more research. I suggest reading *World Wide Web Marketing: Integrating the Web into Your Marketing Strategy* by Jim Sterne, Wiley & Sons.

- Trade shows Whatever your business, there are at least ten trade shows that cater to it. We talked about being a presenter in chapter 4, but now, if you're serious about your business, you should attend a few of these as an exhibitor. It's a great place to check out the competition as well as get some marketing ideas—not to mention meet potential customers and network. From gift shows to cooking expos to book fairs to college activities, there's a show for your company somewhere out there. Do a Google search under "trade shows" in your area of business. A good way to save money is to attend a regional show rather than a national show. You'll save on the booth fees and can still make some great contacts. Make sure you have ample brochures, business cards, and any other literature on hand to give out when people stop by. Since this stuff can get costly, try and find a graphic design student to help you out. Not only will you get very creative stuff, they may even be able to help you find a printing company for less.

- Mailing lists Prepackaged mailing labels are the way to go for direct-mail campaigns. Here, you specify what types of people you're looking to target (lists can be sorted by zip code, household income, or interest, as well as in lots of other ways). You'll pay for a set of labels, which will be mailed to you. There are too many companies to mention offering all kinds of label services combined with direct mail packages. Surf around and see what suits your needs.

- Postcards Self-mailers or postcards are a good way to launch your direct-mail marketing campaign. Try Modern Postcard (www.modernpostcard.com) for fast turnaround at very reasonable prices.

- Help! Consider hiring a college student to help you market your product or service. You'd be surprised how resourceful they are (remember, you were once there!). You can even offer an unpaid (or low paid) internship through area colleges and universities— even high schools. Interns are great for data entry, phone calls, mailings, and other time-consuming tasks, not to mention coffee. I know this because I was one . . . frequently. But *please* be nice to your interns.

And the Number One Free Marketing Resource Is . . .

- Word of mouth! Remember the "turn one person into five" rule from chapter 4? Well, try turning one person into 5,000. Spread the good word and your business will take off. I don't care if you have to hire people to do it (hey, it worked for the Beatles). Get your friends to go nuts telling people about your business. Offer free samples, stand on street corners, call your old ballet teacher, organize free seminars, book readings and theatrical showcases at your local library—pull out all the stops! If you don't have money to spend on a huge marketing campaign, you're going to have to use your mouth. Talk it up, baby.

Additional Business Resources for Entrepreneurs

Catalyst Women
www.catalystwomen.org

Provides a wealth of information and research tools on and for women in business.

National Association of Women Business Owners
www.nawbo.org

Represents the interests of women business owners around the country. Also, a source for contacts and networking.

Small Business Administration
www.sba.gov

Mentioned before, but I'll list it here, too.

www.onlinewbc.gov

Part of the Small Business Administration, here you can find a comprehensive listing of other women's business organizations that may offer networking events in your area.

City-Specific Resources

Atlanta

www.atlanta.bizjournals.com/atlanta/entrepreneur/
The *Atlanta Business Chronicle* has a special section for entrepreneurs and a calendar of local events.

Chicago

www.wehaveanswers.org
Offers resources for entrepreneurs and small business owners; free consulting and workshops in Chicago.

Los Angeles

www.worksourcecalifornia.com
Operated by the Workforce Investment Board, they can supply employees for your business in California.

www.lacity.org/cdd
The City of Los Angeles Community Development Department offers many different business services for everyone from small entrepreneurs to large commercial developers.

New York City

www2.nypl.org/smallbiz/
Offers local resources and small business assistance for entrepreneurs in the New York area.

San Francisco

www.sanfrancisco.bizjournals.com/sanfrancisco/
The *San Francisco Business Times* has a section for entrepreneurs and a calendar of local events.

Part 3

Spare Time

6

~~~~~~~~~~

Take It to the Couch

Some words on mental health

If you're like most women, you've probably thought about therapy at some point in your life. After processing the information from the previous chapters, you're probably thinking about it even more. Not that you have to be like everybody else. But it's worth thinking about, especially if you're feeling depressed on a daily basis, or if there are some real issues getting in the way of moving forward with your life.

Therapy was once taboo and something people only did when they had a serious problem. Today it's so common and diverse, you could go nuts (pardon the pun) trying to figure out the various types. The good thing is—thanks to people like Tipper Gore—the word "therapy" is wide out in the open.

What's important to know before anyone starts playing with your head, however, is that there are different methods of therapy. In some ways, they're kind of like religions. If you don't believe a certain method will help you, it probably won't. Try to use a practicioner with a type that "just makes sense" to you.

In all seriousness, therapy is not something that should be taken lightly. It's time consuming, it's expensive (unless you can get your insurance to pay for it), and it's hard work. Just sitting in there like a lump isn't going to make you better either; therapy doesn't work by osmosis.

How Do I Know If Therapy's Right for Me?

Aside from the fact that most therapists will say everyone could use a little, some situations are more urgent in nature and require immediate attention. Ask yourself the following questions:

- Do I have trouble making a decision?
- Do I cry a lot for no apparent reason?
- Do I feel unfulfilled in my relationships?
- Is my mood erratic and unpredictable?
- Do I obsess over the little things on a regular basis?
- Do I need other people's approval for everything I do?
- Am I an obsessive drinker, drug user, eater, shopper, smoker, sexaholic, gambler, etc?

- Do I constantly find myself in situations that I can't get out of?
- Do I feel the need to please others more than I do myself?
- Do I feel stuck in a troubled relationship, career, or other life situation?
- Am I too competitive with myself?
- Am I unable to interact with people?
- Do I have trouble sleeping or concentrating?
- Am I intensely paranoid to the point where it interferes with my relationships?
- Do I dislike myself?
- Do I worry too much?
- Am I unhappy?

Now, after beating yourself up over these questions, take a deep breath. You probably are surprised at how many you answered "Yes." Yeah, me too. These questions are important and if you did answer yes to more than a few, you should consider talking to a therapist. If you're honest with yourself now, you'll be a lot happier later in life.

Whether you answered yes to one or ten of the above questions, it's important to know about the different types of therapy out there. The last thing you want to do is hook yourself up with a quack. No matter which type you choose, make sure you research the therapist personally. Try to get referrals. You should also know that there are a tremendous number of support groups on all sorts of mental health issues—from sleep disorders to alcoholism—should you want to be with other people who are dealing with a similar issue. In terms of one-on-one help, here's a quick look at some of the most common types of therapies practiced today:

Types of Therapy

Cognitive (Cognitive-Behavioral)

Cognitive therapy has become increasingly popular among young people in recent years. Its practice focuses on the present rather than the past. Based on a more realistic approach to thinking, cognitive therapy teaches short-term problem-solving skills that can be applied to specific life situations. As a result, you change the way in which you perceive, and ultimately respond to, those situations. Don't be surprised if you're given homework to do between sessions that can help speed up your progress. While not a quick fix by any means, treatment generally doesn't last years as with some other therapies.

Best Candidates for Cognitive Therapy

- Those who are goal oriented.
- Those who want to take a hands-on approach to solving their problems.
- Those who may be only affected by one particular situation such as fears, eating disorders, substance abuse, or obsessions. More recently, however, cognitive therapy has also been shown to be effective for co-occurring disorders.

To find a cognitive therapist near you, log on to the Academy of Cognitive Therapy website (www.academyofct.org). They have a low-cost therapist referral program that you can access by typing in your zip code. For additional information on Cognitive/Behavioral Therapy, log on to:

www.beckinstitute.org
www.behavioralhealthassoc.com
In Atlanta: www.cognitiveatlanta.com
In New York: www.cognitivetherapynyc.com

Psychotherapy / Psychoanalysis

Based on Sigmund Freud's belief that all behavior stems from unconscious motivation, psychotherapy conducted by a Freudian-trained analyst is a treatment to understand conflict and problems, with the goal being personality growth, self-awareness, and behavioral change. Treatment can range anywhere from a few months to many years, depending upon the patient and the analyst. The therapy often digs deep into childhood and adolescent events and feelings, even those that the patient may not consciously remember, to understand current problems.

For those who really want to get into it, you may be a candidate for *psychoanalysis*. This is where you get down and dirty and lie on the couch. Psychoanalysts have gone through extensive training as well as years of their own concentrated therapy. The process is a very intensive (and intense) and can last years. It requires an incredible commitment from the patient. But, for those who have gone through it, many swear by it. They believe it has changed their lives.

Best Candidates for Psychoanalysis

- Those who are willing to dedicate a lot of time and energy to getting to the root of the problem and getting in touch with their inner self.
- Those who can talk freely about family and intimate relationships.
- Those who can't quite figure out what's wrong.

Additional information on certain types of psychotherapy and psychoanalysis can be found by contacting the New York Freudian Society Referral Service at 212-873-7029 or by logging on to www.nyfreudian.org.

Psychiatry and Psychology

A psychiatrist is a medical doctor, licensed to treat patients as well as administer medication for mental illness. A psychiatrist has gone through four years of medical school and an additional four-plus years of clinical experience. A clinical psychologist may hold a Sc.D. or a Ph.D., but not an M.D. While both psychiatrists and psychologists are trained in the areas of therapy and mental illness, and have gone through a tremendous amount of schooling, the main difference between the two is that psychologists cannot prescribe medication.

You've probably heard a lot about drugs such as Prozac, Paxil, and Zoloft, in addition to a newer drug now on the market, Lexapro. These are the ones most commonly used to treat depression. Categorized as seratonin specific reuptake inhibitors (SSRI drugs), they increase the amount of seratonin (a neurotransmitter) in the brain, which improves your mood. These drugs are marketed to help people with generalized anxiety disorders, sleep disorders, depression, stress, panic attacks, or obsessive-compulsive disorders. The side effects vary from drug to drug and range from decreased libido to weight gain, increased heart rate, insomnia, and dry mouth. If you feel you need medication to deal with your issues, it is highly recommended that you see a psychiatrist. In addition, any reputable psychologist or other type of therapist will refer you to the appropriate clinician or psychopharmacologist should she feel medication is necessary.

For more information on psychiatry contact the American Psychiatric Association at www.psych.org.

Best Candidates for Psychiatry

- Those who want a more conventional approach to mental health from a medical perspective.
- Those who feel they need drugs to treat a problem.

Best Candidates for Psychology

- Treatment varies depending on the type of psychology practiced by a therapist. Consult the American Psychological Association's website at www.apa.org for a comprehensive listing of therapies.

Social Work

A licensed social worker has a minimum of two years of social work school plus additional work experience in a professional setting. Some social workers may have more experience in clinical settings, hospitals, managed care facilities, schools, or nonprofit organizations. While many social workers also function as therapists, it's up to you to decide if the therapy they provide is adequate. Many social workers are hired by organizations to help clients with practical issues such as job hunting, housing, and filing legal papers. Often by default, however, they act more as therapists and may even see private patients. Social workers' fees typically aren't as astronomical as a psychotherapist's (a trained psychotherapist in NYC can command up to $300 per hour, and just so you know, many have social-work degrees) but then again, they also haven't been through as much training. You may find that a social worker is helpful, depending on your situation and its magnitude.

Best Candidates for Social Work

- Those who may need counseling for practical issues relating to legal, job, financial, family, or housing matters.

- Those who are dealing with terminal illness, emotional problems, or substance abuse and are part of a program in a hospital or other institution. Families of these individuals may also benefit from the social worker's services as well.

- Those who have access to a social worker on-staff at their place of business and find their services adequate to help them work through a difficult period in their lives.

To find a social worker near you, contact the National Association of Social Workers at www.socialworkers.org.

Holistic Therapy

Holistic therapy looks at the individual as a whole in relation to her surroundings. Areas of particular focus are the senses: sight, smell, sound, and touch. Often combined with alternative treatments such as acupuncture, acupressure, aromatherapy, or herbal remedies, holistic therapy may also employ music, dance, art, or animals (it's not what you're thinking) as part of the treatment process. While unconventional in nature, holistic therapy is becoming increasingly popular. For those who choose this route, it's important to note that holistic therapy is not supported by many medical professionals. This doesn't mean it can't work for you, but as with all therapy, you should be extra cautious when choosing your therapist. Be wary of those who promise miracles or make unrealistic claims. Find out if your therapist is known in your community, or if he has written any papers for scientific journals. Do your research. A great place to start is with the National Institutes of Health. Log on to www.nlm.nih.gov/medlineplus/alternativemedicine.html.

Best Candidates for Holistic Therapy

- Those who are looking for an unconventional approach to treating their problems.
- Those who've had success with acupuncture, acupressure, or other similar treatments.

Art, Dance, and Music Therapies

I grouped these together because they all basically have the same philosophy behind them. Use your creative inner self to figure out what is wrong with you. And you can kill two birds with one stone here: fix your head while taking an art class.

I'm not joking. By listening to music, drawing a picture, or participating in some sort of creative expression, the therapist uses art to connect with the patient's emotions.

You'll find many music, art, and dance therapists employed in hospitals working with children who can only communicate using creative expression. But it's known to work well for adults, too. So, if you're interested in learning more, check out these organizations:

www.arttherapy.org
www.musictherapy.org

Best Candidates for Art, Music, or Dance Therapy

- Those who are seeking creative approaches to mental health.
- Those whose current treatment may also recommend using art, dance, or music as a means of expression.

Clergy

Sometimes a good dose of the cloth is all you need. If you're going through a specific period of difficulty (such as divorce, death in the family, relationship woes, etc.) and feel a connection to a particular religious institution, you may want to talk with your priest, minister, or rabbi. Clergy are trained in social services as well as theology. And, best of all, it won't cost you a dime.

Best Candidates for Clergy

- Those who are figuring out where to turn for help. Clergy are sometimes a good first stop.
- Those who can't afford to pay for any type of therapy.
- Those who are involved in their church, temple, or synagogue and feel comfortable in a religious setting.

Interviewing a Therapist

It was hard enough convincing yourself you had to go—now what happens if you don't like your choice? Well, you'll have to shop around, just like with anything else. It can get a little tricky, but you need to feel confident with your therapist before you start the hard work.

Some therapists are like gyms. You get locked into so many sessions that nothing short of your own death can get you out of it. Since this is probably something you want to avoid (which is why you came to therapy in the first place), you're going to have to decide if your therapy is working for you and *then* decide to stick with it or not. Don't mistake hard work for not liking your therapist. There'll be days when you absolutely hate her—but this doesn't mean it's not working. Only you will be able to judge the effectiveness of the treatment, so be honest with yourself. If you truly feel the therapy isn't making you think a little differently about yourself at all by the fifth or sixth session, you may want to consider trying someone else. Just be prepared to be firm with your therapist so you don't spend your hour analyzing why you're choosing to go elsewhere.

When you do go to your first session, here are some questions you may want to ask:

- Where did you do your training?
- How does your type of therapy work?
- When will I notice changes in myself?
- Do you offer a payment plan (sometimes called a sliding scale)?
- Can you give me a few references?

Paying for Therapy

Most health insurance plans have a mental-health division that can refer you to a host of mental-health clinicians. But they'll only send you a list, not a personal recommendation. If you go through your employer's insurance, the human resources department will know you're getting therapy. If you don't want your employer to know this, you may opt to bypass reporting your treatment to your insurance. But this also means that you will have to pay out of pocket—and that can get costly. Average fees for therapists range from $50 to well over $250 an hour, depending on your city and specialist. One thing you should always do up front is ask your therapist about payment plans. Many will work with you if you're on a tight budget and reduce their fees to accommodate your needs. This may be especially true for a budding therapist fresh out of training. Many are eager to start a practice, and you'd be surprised how skilled they are.

Additional Therapy Resources

Any college or university in your area will have resources on affordable mental health providers in your area. You may not be able to visit an on-campus clinic if you're not affiliated with the institution, but it's always worth a call to find out for sure.

Also, you can get a host of information about specific anxiety disorders from the Anxiety Disorders Association of America (www.adaa.org).

City-Specific Resources

Chicago

Access Community Health Network
www.accesscommunityhealth.net
866-882-2237

Over forty health-center organizations throughout Chicago providing health care, regardless of your ability to pay.

The Medical Group
773-978-5700

Confidential services for women, including counseling; public aid and student discounts available.

Los Angeles

The Los Angeles Free Clinics
www.lafreeclinic.org
323-653-1990

Beverly Clinic
Hollywood Center
Hollywood Wilshire

These clinics offer a wide range of affordable (and some free) health-care services and resources.

New York City

Center for Educational and Psychological Services
Teachers College—Columbia University
www.tc.edu/ceps
212-678-3262

Fees range from $5 to $40. You'll see graduate students trained in all areas of therapy.

National Institute for the Psychotherapies (NIP)
www.nipinst.org
212-582-1566

Offers reduced fees for students and those who are unemployed with proof of financial status.

San Francisco

Therapy Network
www.therapynetwork.net
415-974-9779 (San Francisco and Marin)
510-287-9225 (East Bay)

A not-for-profit organization offering referrals for psychotherapists for women, couples, and families.

Washington, D.C.

D.C. Department of Mental Health
35 K Street NE
202-442-4215
1125 Spring Road NW
202-576-6513

Individual and group therapy on a sliding-scale basis.

George Washington University
2300 M Street NW Suite 910
202-887-0775

Receive therapy on a sliding-scale from clinical psychology doctoral candidates under supervision from university faculty.

Community Connections
www.communityconnectionsdc.org
202-546-1512

Multiple locations in the D.C. area offer a variety of support programs.

7

〰〰〰〰〰〰

Dating Yourself

Creative ways
to spend time
on your own

We've all been there: mateless. It's especially annoying when your girlfriends are planning their weddings and you're supposed to be happy for them, but all you can think about is the fact that you're going to be thirty (okay, so maybe its in five years) and you don't even have a boyfriend. That means you've got a year to find one, a year of courtship, a year of planning the wedding, and—assuming you didn't have a shotgun—you'll want at least two years to be with the guy before you have kids. Which makes you, like, fifty before you're going to have a baby—and that's too old! Deep breath. It's okay. More women are having kids later in life these days. Some of them grandma age! First of all, it's not that bad. Second of all, there's more to life than meeting someone. I mean, look at the divorce rate—to the moon. And if you ask me, there's only one reason for it. People aren't happy with themselves. And, like many of our parents, nobody had time to figure it out before they met their mate. So look at it as a chance to change the stats. Read this chapter carefully. Go out on your own now and have fun with yourself, so when you do find someone, you're already content! And that brings me to dating yourself.

Dating yourself is actually pretty fun. You can basically pick anything you want to do and don't have to deal with someone else's opinion about how to do it. Think movies, shows, museums, and restaurants—even overnight trips, if you're daring. The first time I went to a restaurant alone (okay, the first few times), I put a book by the other seat to make it look like someone was joining me. But I got over it. Now I walk in with confidence, not caring what the hostess thinks. I order wine, appetizers, a full entrée—even dessert. Yep. I go to a movie, I get a large tub of popcorn and eat it by myself. Sometimes I go for the free refill. Now that I'm married (yes, I did finally get married), I still go out alone. It's something I've learned to cherish. And it's fun. *Really*. You're not a loser if you go out by yourself. You're *cool!* And you're more likely to get a ticket to a hot concert or show as a single than a couple.

The art of dating yourself is really something you should do if you're single *or* in a relationship. It's about feeling comfortable walking into a restaurant or a movie alone, or just exploring your own interests. It's also the best way to avoid pining over someone who's not calling you and a good way to keep yourself busy with plans on the weekends.

But just so you don't have to put any more thought into this than you want to, here are some suggestions for great solo dates, all affordably priced (hey, who's picking up the tab here?), of course.

The Dates

The Equestrian (A Day Date)

Start with a hearty breakfast at the local diner. Go for the gusto: eggs, bacon, grits (if you live down South), toast, and a glass of juice. Wait half an hour—just like with swimming—and then head down to the horse stables for a riding lesson. And there are no excuses for you city folk, either. See the list at the end of the chapter for suggestions.

The Poet

Literature and latté, my two favorite combinations. Since you can't take coffee into the library, why not spend the evening at your favorite bookstore? Not only is this a fun place to people-watch, but it's free (well, not the latté)! Whether you want to search for a classic novel, read up on a hobby, or scan every magazine on the racks for a new haircut, you'll lose track of time and have a pleasant solo evening. There's just something about bookstores at night. Personally, I like the independents. Find one in your city by logging on to www.bookweb.org/bookstores/. Lots of public libraries also offer free book clubs, too.

The Tiger

Nothing like a little driving range to get your juices flowing. I love hitting a golf ball (that is, when I can hit it). It's clean, it's fun, and it's really cheap. You can find a driving range in most any city. Buckets of balls generally range from $4 to $20, depending on where you live.

The Scavenger

Antiquing, renovating, stripping (furniture), or discount tchotchke shopping . . . even if you've got money to spare, if you're like me you're always looking for a deal. Your date begins by seeking out flea markets, antique shops, or garage sales in the Friday paper and spending your Saturday searching for finds. It's amazing what you can do with a piece of sandpaper and some polyurethane. In addition to the flea markets listed in chapter 1, you'll find some fun day trips near major cities listed at the end of this chapter.

The Animal Lover

Adopt a pet for the weekend. Before you can even utter "But I don't have the money," consider adopting a Seeing Eye Dog in training. All you have to do is prove you're normal, then provide shelter and food for two days. No hassles, no commitment. Call your local Humane Society to find out if this program is offered near you.

The Bounty Hunter

This is a fun activity, even if you haven't just broken up with someone. Not that I recommend this on a weekly basis, but every now and then a firing range is just what a girl making it on her own needs (and no, I'm not a card-carrying member of the NRA). If you don't like guns, you can also try going to an archery range. Personally, I find it's not as gratifying, but at least you can practice your aim. Check the listings at the end of the chapter for locations.

The Chef

Cooking classes are a great way to explore your own creativity, meet some new people, and enjoy delicious food. You can find these offered at many local colleges or universities under their continuing-education programs, as well as in fine restaurants or culinary institutes. And you don't have to spend a lot of money, either. You'll find some inexpensive city options listed at the end of the chapter.

The Pretend Race-Car Driver

Admit it, you've always wanted to drive a stick shift but you don't know how. Well, now's your chance to learn. You sat there at the arcade playing Turbo just so you could move that stupid thing around, didn't you? I did, and, uh, it didn't exactly work. But after crashing two of my friend's cars, I finally learned. And let me tell you something: not only is driving a stick one hundred times more fun than driving an automatic, but you'll feel empowered beyond your wildest dreams. Find someone to lend you her car (don't borrow the BMW), or rent a wreck (www.rentawreck. com) for the weekend and learn.

The Shopper

Did you think I'd leave this one out? Nothing helps to pass the time more than getting a great deal on a hot outfit. From sample sales to funky boutiques, spend an evening in the dressing room, even if you're just going home afterwards and changing back into your PJs. You'll find great deals at the stores listed at the end of this chapter. For furniture finds, see chapter 1.

The Exercise Freak

The time you spend working out in your twenties and thirties is likely going to be the most time you'll ever have to exercise, especially if you plan to get married and have kids later on. So take advantage of it now! Not only will you feel good after you get on a regular gym roll, but it's a great way to spend half a Saturday or an evening after work. Fancier clubs will have more bells and whistles, such as pools, spas, and fluffy towels, but you'll get the same results from a budget gym without shelling out so much cash. Be sure to check the gym listings at the end of the chapter. A word about gym memberships from big chains: never pay the first initiation fee quoted to you. These are reserved for the suckers. Always tell the sales rep to cut it in half. Nine out ten times he will.

Solo Party Hosting

For those of you who absolutely cannot go out alone, there are other ways to have a good time. One of them is to throw a party for no reason at all. Yes, yes, the thought of hosting people alone for any type of event is frightening. But just because you work hard and live alone doesn't mean you can't be the belle of your own ball. Throwing a party solo can be loads of fun. It's a chance to say "I don't need a mate to have an event." And it'll give you something to look forward to—believe me, we all need that. In terms of reasons to have a party, do you really need one? No, but it's always fun. Here are some ideas for you to try:

Singles Mixer

Have each of your friends bring someone who's single. Don't try to mix and match here—just let the evening unfold on its own.

What to serve: Hey, if you're not mixing and matching guests, why not mix and match food? Try the nacho cheese dip and stir fry up some frozen veggie dumplings. Serve with a pitcher of sangria. Or, have everyone bring one person and one dish—just make sure they don't all bring the same dish (or the same person).

Tea Party

This is a really nice afternoon party for the ladies. You can make a variety of teas and serve with milk, honey, or caramel. Be creative with sandwiches and desserts. Ask your guests to wear funky hats.

What to serve: Cucumber and Alouette cheese spread on white bread cut up in triangles (no crusts, please), pretzels in honey mustard sauce, party ryes with lox spread. Anything dainty works, just make a lot so you don't starve!

Murder Mystery Party

A fun alternative to typical New Year's Eve mayhem. There are a few board games out there that orchestrate an entire murder mystery evening. Find some great ones on www.areyougame.com. Buy the game beforehand and tell your guests to dress the part. Dinner can also be part of the theme.

> What to serve: A murder in a Tuscan villa calls for pasta and lots of red wine, while a mystery on the Nile can be combined with a Middle Eastern feast of hummus, salads, pita, and chicken kabobs. Don't be afraid to get a little wacky. Then again, you can always order Chinese.

PJ Party with Masseuse

Everybody loves getting a massage. Stop by your local nail salon and find out how much they would charge to send a masseuse up to your place for a few hours of manicures and massages for your gal pals. For some reason, this is really cheap in cities like New York and Los Angeles, perhaps due to the overwhelming number of nail salons. It's also a fun way to host a bridal shower, birthday, or end a really stressful week at work.

> What to Serve: Anything on a stick so you don't mess up your nails.

Remodeling Party

Like the show *Trading Spaces*? Why not create your own version? Maybe you've always wanted to redecorate, but just don't have the "touch." Invite your friends for an assessment and demolition party, get rid of the junk and figure out what you can salvage. Paint, stencil, and sand away. Give each friend a job and let them each use their talents to make your pad a little more spiffy. Note: this party is not a good idea if you are a control freak.

> What to serve: Trade recipes. Have each of your friends bring a dish and the recipe that goes along with it.

I Hate the Superbowl but Love the Food Party

This is where you put the Superbowl on low so that it *looks* like you're watching, but truly the only reason you're getting everyone together is so that you can eat chips, dips, and pigs in blankets with a purpose. For those who want to actually watch, have a TV set up in another room, but keep the real partying focused around the food.

What to serve: Velveeta dip, pigs-in-blankets, potato skins, baked Brie, beer. Anything fattening and cheap.

I Got Rejected Party!

This can also be done as an I Got Fired Party, I got Laid Off Party, I Got Laid Off *Again* Party, I got Dumped Party, etc. This is where you say "Screw it" to convention and lack of money. Just go ahead and indulge! Have everything you've ever wanted but couldn't eat because of Atkins on one plate: peanut butter cups, ice cream and hot fudge, high-fat potato chips, real sour cream and onion dip, and double cheese pizza. Don't forget lots of wine and maybe even a few Jell-O shots for old times sake. There's no organization to this party—just sheer madness. Invite your friends over and allow your cute little apartment to become a total dump. Take out your aggressions on the food, the alcohol, the guy your friend brought—just make sure you've got people to help you clean up the next day. Your true friends will stay. When the eating's done, have some down pillows on hand for an all-out pillow fight—one final stage of aggression. Make sure the feathers go everywhere, even in the dip. The place should look like a sty when you're done. If you're really nervous, then hide the important stuff and cover the floor with garbage bags first. This is what I did—uh, I mean what I'd do.

I'm Not Cool Enough for the OC or Sex and the City Party

This is where you and your friends wear the sexiest possible outfit you can find in your own closet and then see how it matches up (or doesn't) to the babes from these shows. Make your own cocktails and pretend you can actually get into a bar like Marquee in Manhattan. Then, compare cellulite and eat some more chips.

Some of the best parties are simply the ones thrown together at the last minute. Don't feel as if you have to have everyone under the sun, either. Small, intimate groups where everyone contributes something are always nice. When you're working, it's always the last-minute stuff that takes the most time. Have each friend bring something easy, but something that you don't need to deal with: A loaf of bread, olives, salsa and chips, dessert. Give people categories and you'll cover your bases. Oftentimes I'll take care of the main course and have my friends bring the rest. They still feel like they're being entertained, but I don't have to worry about accessorizing with side dishes. The recipes at the end of the chapter can help you out.

Party Supplies

You don't need to go crazy with drinks and decorations, but it'll help to have some sort of creative stuff around the place if you're throwing a bash.

- Centerpieces Don't spend money on these. Having a fall party? Throw a pumpkin in the middle of the table and grab some leaves off your street (or the park) and sprinkle around.

- Christmas or holiday party? Buy a $3 bag of red and green confetti, or sprinkle some Hanukkah gelt around the table for a festive look. I highly recommend taking full advantage of the 99 cent store if there's one near you. They've got candles galore, which always make a place look festive.

- Summer bash Buy a few blow-up beach balls at the drug store and toss them around your apartment. You can also buy a few packs of children's sunglasses and put them on your serving trays with summer fruits to garnish.

- Party favors? Fuhgeddaboudit.

- Alcohol This is where so many parties get costly. Some advice: Ask your guests to bring the booze. Hey, you're taking care of the food and venue; they can throw in a bottle of wine, for crying out loud. Ten guests, seven bottles (got to assume some people will forget). But if you just have to do it all yourself, the answer is: *buy in bulk*. So what if it's cheap wine—just throw in some orange and apple slices and make sangria. That way it'll mask the taste of the cheapness. Costco, Sam's Club, BJ's—they've got it all. See what I'm talking about? You don't need a $20 bottle of Chardonnay—get the $7 bottle and throw some seltzer and a lime in it. Can you spell s-p-r-i-t-z-e-r? Let one of your friends be on mixer duty. This'll keep you free to meet and greet your guests. Another idea is to bag the bar altogether and go with a punch bowl. This way, you can jazz up even the cheapest alcohol with some fruit, Hi-C, and a decorative ice ring (see recipe later). Put some vodka, Sprite, and any kind of red juice into a big bowl and throw in an ice ring. You'll have just classed up your college punch!

- Just say no to the preassembled platter Whatever you do, *do not* buy these. For every veggie sliced and diced on a plastic plate, that's an extra $.50 out of your pocket. Grab a bag of chopped up broccoli and carrots at the grocery store, alternate colors, and throw a sour cream dip in the middle.

- Use online invites You'll save on stamps and stationery by sending out EVITES (www.evite.com). They're fast and free and you can keep tabs on your guests from work when you're sneaking personal computer time.

- Photos Get your friend in art school to take black and white photos of the party. This will make you look cool and artsy. If you want live music, contact a local music school in your area and hire a student or two to play. They'll love the exposure and won't charge you much.

Still nervous about throwing a party on your own? Down a few of your own Jell-O shots before your guests arrive and let the festivities begin! You deserve this night!

Solo Travel

To take going out alone a step further, the concept of traveling solo is getting more exciting by the day. Pick a passion: cooking, hiking, mountain biking or hang gliding, and you'll have your pick of companies catering to the solo traveler—more specifically, the solo female traveler. Here are some resources to get you started:

- **JourneyWoman** Offers a wealth of information for any woman traveling alone (or in a group) such as trip suggestions, safety measures, and advice from solo women travelers around the globe. www.journeywoman.com

- **REI Adventures** Offers a wide range of adventure trips for women. Not cheap by any means, but if you can splurge a little, you'll be in good hands. Log on to: www.rei.com/adventures and click on the "Women's Travel" section.

- **Contiki Vacations** Caters to 18–35-years-olds and lists specials for last-minute travelers. This is a fun group to try if you like to party.

- **Alpenhutte Lodge** Located in Colorado, the Alpenhutte offers affordable lodge packages catering to the solo traveler. Choose from dorm-style or private rooms. www.alpenhutte.com

- **Great Adventure People** Offering small-group tours to independent travelers, this Canadian company runs trips worldwide on the cheap. Looking to escape for a while? Try a 46-day trip throughout Mexico and Central America that runs less than $2000 for starters. www.gap.ca

- **Mount Tremblant** You can get a fab spa package and your own condo at this Canadian mountain retreat located two hours north of Montreal, especially if you go off-season in the summer. www.clubtremblant.com

- **Web fares** Spend five minutes logging on to a few airlines' websites and sign up for their last-minute fares (may also be called fares or e-savers). Every week you'll get a list of the last-minute weekend specials with fares around $150. One note, you may have to fly back on a Monday to get the deal, so plan your trip accordingly.

- Site59 This is a fantastic resource for last-minute vacation specials. Choose from a variety of flight, hotel, and car packages around the world at affordable prices. www.site59.com

- Travelzoo Sign up for their Top 20 list and get the latest deals and steals e-mailed to you on hot airfares and hotel packages. www.travelzoo.com

- Priceline You've wanted to try it but you're too scared, right? Well, it's good! If you're afraid to book the flight because you don't want to wind up changing planes five times, at least try it for the car rental or hotel. You can choose the level of accommodations you want in the city of your choice (sorry, you can't pick the hotel by name) and put in a suggested amount. Be careful. Once you commit to a price, your credit card will be charged. Be realistic, too—you only get a few chances for the computer to accept your bid. For more information, log on to www.priceline.com. But trust me here. This is a fantastic way to save money and score on five-star accommodations!

- Hotwire.com Like Priceline, but you don't have to guess the lowest price—the site tells you how low it will go, but not what airline or what time of day you'll fly.

Surviving the Holidays on Your Own

But alas, all vacations can't be surf and sun, ski lodges and hot cocoa. Yes, you will one day have to return home and deal with your relatives and their barrage of questions. And so, here are suggestions for how to respond to Aunt Edna and the like while sitting around your Thanksgiving table.

What to Say When They're Really Bugging You

IF YOUR FAMILY SAYS . . .	YOUR RESPONSE IS . . .
Why aren't you seeing anyone?	I'm too busy sleeping around to date anybody seriously
Did you get the job yet?	No, but I've been asked back to two interviews at Hooters. And now that they have an airline, think of the potential to move up the corporate ladder!
How long do you think you'll be able to pull this off?	As long as Mr. President keeps extending unemployment, I think I'll be in great shape.
You think it's safe to live alone?	I paid off the drunk on my stoop so he makes sure no one follows me home.
You know, (insert neighbor's name)'s daughter took a great job here. I'm sure she could introduce you to some nice people.	Nah. (They'll be waiting for you to say something else but you won't—really throws 'em for a loop.)
When do you think you'll move back home?	Once they clear my police record, I should be good to go.
It's just so hard out there. Why don't you just come back home and live with us?	Only if I can turn the guest bedroom back into my bedroom and put pin-ups of Jon Bon Jovi on the walls. (They'll renege on the offer immediately, since they just painted.)
What happens if you get hurt?	I'll be fine, really. My neighbor plays a nurse on ER.
You must be lonely up there with no friends.	Who could be lonely with Tivo?
You know, I could call my friend Sylvia's cousin who has a nice nephew who works near you. He's very smart.	That's okay, thanks so much. It's actually a really small town and I met Matthew (make up name) already. We went out for drinks and wound up drunk in his apartment. I'd really feel awkward if Sylvia found out about it. You know how those things are, right, Grandma?

Some More Realistic Options

If eggnog and Christmas music make you want to hole up because you're just not where you thought you'd be at this time in your life, here are some additional (and more practical) suggestions to make the season a little more tolerable.

- Pick one holiday party—just one. Tell yourself it'll be the only one you'll go to during the season. Make a promise to yourself that you'll at least try to have a good time. Then, kindly decline the other invites (unless of course it's a work party you have to attend) and make other plans.

153

- **Stay away from the mall** Right around October 31, somebody somewhere decides it's time to start the Santa music. And while it's nice to hear for about a week, come December you're just about ready to strangle that somebody. The point of the matter is: Do your holiday shopping early so you don't have to get more depressed going to the mall, fighting off the crowds and hearing that blasted holiday music, which reminds you why you're depressed in the first place!

- **Volunteer** One of the greatest ways to spend the holidays alone is to serve someone who's less fortunate than you. Not only will you feel good about yourself, you'll probably meet a few really nice people who may have similar thoughts to you about the holiday season. Call your local church, synagogue, or community center to find out what holiday volunteer opportunities exist. In New York, try New York Cares (www.nycares.org). In Chicago, try Chicago Volunteer (www.chicagovolunteer.net). And in Los Angeles, try Volunteers of America (www.voala.org). You can also do this through local community centers and religious organizations.

- **Cook yourself a feast and rent a classic movie** This is a favorite activity of mine on New Year's Eve. I cook something that I would never eat the rest of the year (lamb; London broil; some sort of white, flaky fish) and rent something in black and white. It's the ultimate escape and a lot of fun. Pick up a copy of *Solo Suppers: Simple Delicious Meals to Cook for Yourself* by Joyce Esersky Goldstein, Chronicle Books, for some tasty recipes.

- **Treat yourself to a massage or a facial** Find out if there's an aesthetic training institute in your city and book yourself a facial! You'll pay next to nothing for a high quality treatment from a student in training. Check out www.aveda.com for a list of Aveda Training Institutes in your city.

- **Get lost in a book** Reading is a great way to lose track of time. Pick up a new memoir or get a recommendation from the librarian on a fun holiday read.

- **Clean** Cleaning is a good way to let off steam. When you're done, you'll also have a great end result. If the holidays get you down, turn up the tunes and go to town with the Lysol.

- **Promises, shmomises** So you didn't quite lose that ten pounds you said you would last New Year's Eve. Big deal! Give yourself a break and pat yourself on the back for just being able to get out of bed and make it to work in the morning.

Easy Party Recipes

Baked Brie

You'll need: 1 Brie wheel, 1 package Pillsbury Crescent Rolls
Prep Time: 2 minutes to unroll and wrap, 15 minutes to bake
Directions: Unroll crescent rolls into a big square (don't break off at dotted lines) and lay Brie wheel inside. Wrap sides up around cheese and pull off extra pieces that are too long. Bake at 300 degrees for ten minutes or until top is brown and bubbly. Mmmm . . .

Spinach Dip

You'll need: 1 package frozen spinach, 1 package Knorr's Vegetable Soup Mix, 1 cup mayo, 1 cup sour cream
Prep time: 10 minutes
Directions: Thaw, rinse, and dry spinach. Mix everything together. Chill for at least 2 hours before serving.

Pigs in Blankets

You'll need: 1 pack of hot dogs, Pillsbury Crescent Rolls (if you make the Baked Brie, you can use the remaining pieces from the crescent rolls)
Prep time: 15 minutes
Directions: Cut hot dogs into bite-size pieces. Wrap bits of crescent rolls around the pieces, leaving ends of hot dogs sticking out. Bake for 10–12 minutes at 350 degrees. Serve with mustard.

Stuffed 'Shrooms

You'll need: mushrooms, bread crumbs, chopped onion, garlic, celery, and whatever other veggies you have in the drawer, olive oil, salt and pepper, Parmesan cheese
Prep time: 20 minutes
Directions: Wash and take the stems off the mushrooms. Put stems in a bowl. Chop onion, garlic, and celery into tiny pieces (or mince if you have a blender) along with mushroom stems. Stuff this mixture into the mushroom caps and top with Parmesan cheese. Drizzle with olive oil and bake at 350 degrees until golden brown (about 15 minutes).

Hummus

You'll need: hummus
Prep time: none (1 minute if you put it in your own dish)
Directions: Just buy it pre-made and serve with pita bread.

Mexican Layer Dip

You'll need: 1 package shredded cheddar cheese, 1 container
prepackaged guacamole, 1 container sour cream, 1 can bean dip, 1
can sliced black olives, bag of tortilla chips
Prep time: 10 minutes
Directions: Layer everything one by one in a round dish, starting with
the bean dip, guacamole, sour cream, cheese, and olives. Serve with
tortilla chips.

Ridiculously Easy Cheese Dip

You'll need: 1 block Velveeta cheese, 1 jar of salsa
Prep time: 5 minutes
Directions: This is so easy you'll laugh. Put the block of Velveeta into
a bowl and dump in the salsa. Microwave for 2–3 minutes, or until
cheese melts. Mix and serve. Your guests will be astounded at the
flavor and think you spent hours on this recipe. If cheese dip gets
cold, just stick it back in the microwave.

Hot Hors d'oeuvres

You'll need: One word—Costco. Buy Wiltons hors d'oeuvres in the
frozen food section. You can't go wrong with these things. You'll get a
box of little spinach pies, puff pastries, and mushroom thingies all in
one box.
Prep time: 10–15 minutes (all baking time)
Directions: Open box. Throw everything on a cookie sheet and bake
according to directions.

Brunch Ideas

Pasta Salad

You'll need: 1 box of shaped pasta, 1 jar of Italian dressing, cut up
vegetables
Prep time: 15 minutes

Directions: Cook pasta according to directions. Toss with cut up veggies and Italian dressing. Chill until serving time.

Quiche

You'll need: Quiche
Prep time: 15–20 minutes (bake time)
Directions: Buy a frozen one and bake as directed. You see where I'm going here?

Omelettes

You'll need: eggs, scallions, shredded cheddar cheese, mushrooms, peppers, black beans, sour cream, salsa
Prep time: 20 minutes
Directions: Put each topping in a bowl on the table. Have your guests pick the combo they want and make an omelette. You remember how to cook eggs, right? If you can't do the omelette flip (I can't), just do a scramble. It tastes better anyway.

Desserts

Ice Cream Sundaes

You'll need: 2 gallons ice cream, whipped cream, sprinkles, cherries, hot fudge
Prep time: 5 minutes
Directions: Promote this as a "make your own sundae" event.

Hello Dollies

You'll need: 1 stick butter, 1 can condensed milk, 1 cup graham cracker crumbs, 1 cup chocolate chips, 1 cup shredded coconut.
Prep time: 8 minutes prep, 30 minutes bake time
Directions: Melt butter in bottom of 8"x 8" pan. Layer on top: crumbs, chocolate chips, and coconut. Pour can of condensed milk on top and bake at 350 degrees for 30 minutes or until fork comes out clean. Cool and cut into squares.

Cookies with Kisses

You'll need: 1 package cookie dough (the ones sold in square chunks in the dairy section), 1 package Hershey's Kisses, mini muffin tin
Prep time: 5 minutes (bake time 10 minutes)

Directions: Spray muffin tin with non-stick spray. Put 1 block of cookie dough in each hole and bake for 8 minutes. Remove from oven and place a Hershey's Kiss in the middle of each cookie. Bake for an additional 2 minutes. Let cool for 5 minutes and serve warm.

Drinks

Sangria

You'll need: 1 bottle red wine; cut up oranges, apples, and/or peaches; Sprite or 7-Up
Prep time: 5 minutes
Directions: Pour wine into a pitcher. Add Sprite or 7-Up to wine to taste. Add cut up fruit and chill. This looks especially nice in a clear pitcher!

Champagne Punch

You'll need: 1 bottle Sprite or 7-Up, 1 bottle cheap sparkling wine, sorbet (any flavor), plastic Jell-O mold pan for ice ring, strawberries
Prep time: 10 minutes (make the ice ring the day before)
Directions: For ice ring, wash and take stems off of strawberries. Fill Jell-O mold with water and drop in strawberries. Freeze overnight. For champagne punch; combine wine and Sprite or 7-Up in a clear bowl. Add 5 or 6 scoops of sorbet and toss in ice ring as a finishing touch.

City-Specific Resources
Can be done with or without a date

Atlanta

The Equestrian

Chastain Stables at Chastain Park
4371 Powers Ferry Road
404-257-1470

The Tiger

City Golf Academy
Driving Range
2400 Defoors Ferry Road
404-351-5331
$8 for 60 balls / $11 for 100 balls

The Scavenger

Lakewood Antique Market
www.lakewoodantiques.com

Check out this market located on the Lakewood Fairgrounds for an eclectic collection of antiques.

The Bounty Hunter

Tom Lowe Olympic Shooting Grounds
3025 Merk Road SW
404-346-8382

Trap and skeet shooting.

The Chef

Cooks Warehouse
www.cookswarehouse.com
549-I Amsterdam Ave. NE
404-815-4993

Among their numerous classes, the Spanish *Tapas* Party, The Rustic Italian Farmhouse Supper, and the Hot Tamales class run for $45 each.

The Shopper

Fabrik
1114 West Peachtree Street
404-881-8223
You, too, can look like you stepped off the *OC* set, for a fraction of what they'd pay. Very chic fashions at very affordable prices. Make sure you ask about weekend Pilates classes too!

The Fickle Manor
1402-4 North Highland Avenue
404-541-0960
Trendy clothing with good deals found at trunk shows and special events.

The Exercise Freak
Most gym memberships in Atlanta are fairly reasonable, but I'll list one here that's fairly popular:

LA Fitness
www.lafitness.com
Cheap and accessible, these gyms are all over the place.

Absolutely Free in Atlanta

Piedmont Park
Located in town, this expansive park has undergone a major renovation in the last few years.

Chastain Park
Both parks boast acres of green space and trails, though Piedmont is more convenient to those living in town.

Greenways and Paths
Log onto www.pathfoundation.org for a list of winding trails great for biking, running, walking, and blading, woven throughout the city. Here you'll find the Silver Comet trail, which runs all the way from Georgia to the Alabama border.

Boston

The Equestrian

Boston Equestrian Center
44 McIntyre Road
North Oxford, MA
508-987-6141
A short drive from Boston.

The Tiger

Franklin Park Golf Course
1 Circuit Drive
Dorchester, MA
617-265-4084

Just outside of Boston in Dorchester. Take the Orange Line Subway Train to
Forest Hills Station. Board the #16 bus.

The Scavenger

Spending a day in Essex will clear your head of all worries. While accessible via
commuter rail, it's best to borrow a car for this thirty-mile ride outside of the
city. Take route 93N to 128N toward Gloucester. Get off at the first Essex exit.

The Chef

Elephant Walk
www.elephantwalk.com
900 Beacon Street
Boston, MA
617-247-1500

2067 Massachusetts Avenue
Cambridge, MA
617-492-6900

Learn the tricks to tantalizing Cambodian and French cuisine with
unique grilling and spice techniques, at $69 per class. Locations in
Boston and Cambridge.

The Shopper

Filene's Basement (the original, not the chains)
426 Washington Street (at Downtown Crossing)
617-542-2011

Your discount will be based on when an item first went on sale. Much
better than the chains in other cities, and much better deals, too.

Absolutely Free in Boston

You can spend hours along the Charles River esplanade. Here you'll find
close to 20 miles of paved path perfect for biking, blading, running, and
people-watching. Grassy parks line the paths, too. Also a great place to
watch the rowers (especially during the Head of the Charles regatta—
one of the best free events in Boston) or catch a Boston Pops concert
under the Hatch. The esplanade is part of the chain of over 1,000 acres
of parkland called the Emerald Necklace that stretches across the greater
Boston area.

If you can't afford to do the Cape in the summer, spend some time at some of Boston's revitalized beaches, including Carson, M. Street and Pleasure Bay, and Castle Island. For those concerned about the water quality, check out the reports listed in Boston Metro every Friday during the summer, put out by the Massachusetts Water Resource Authority. Or log on to the Boston Harbor Association (www.tbha.org) for updated information.

Chicago

The Equestrian

Glen Grove Equestrian Center
9453 Harris Road (at Golf Road)
Morton Grove, IL (15 miles outside of Chicago)
847-966-8032

The Tiger

Diversey Driving Range
141 W. Diversey Parkway
312-742-7929
$7 for small bucket / $10.50 for large bucket

The Scavenger

Chicago Southland offers a row of antiquing in five historic communities: Blue Island, Beecher, Crete, Frankfort, and Orland Park. You'll wind up spending the entire day in this quaint area. If you choose to stay inside the city limits, try the Chicago Antique Market at 47 West Division, open May through October on the last Sunday of each month.

The Bounty Hunter

West Chicago Trap and Skeet Shooting Club
West Chicago, IL
630-231-9862

The Chef

Cooking Academy of Chicago
www.cookingacad.com
2500 West Bradley Place
773-478-9840

Offers mini classes on topics such as sauces, soups, and bread making for not a lot of cash.

The Chopping Block
www.thechoppingblock.net
1324 West Webster
4747 North Lincoln Avenue.
773-472-6700

Classes are available nearly every day at both locations on meals across a variety of cuisines. Most classes are $50.

The Shopper

Sales Check
Sign up at www.chicagomag.com for Sales Check and receive a weekly email on retail sales, trunk shows, events, and openings.

McShane's Exchange
815 West Armitage Avenue
1141 West Webster Avenue
773-525-0282

Get a deal on gently worn quality clothing and accessories

Daisy Shop
67 East Oak Street, 6th Floor
312-943-8880

A fun Gold Coast shop that sells gently worn couture clothing.

Fox's
2150 North Halsted Street
773-281-0700

Lincoln Park shop with designer clothes at great discounts. There are Fox's in New York, Connecticut, and Florida, too.

The Exercise Freak

Lincoln Park Fitness
www.lpfitness.com
444 West Fullerton Avenue
773-281-8715

A bare-bones, one-room gym, but the monthly fee is pretty cheap, plus there's no registration fee.

Webster Fitness Center
www.websterfitness.com
957 West Webster
773-248-2006

A fun gym that claims to be the cheapest around and the "last of the neighborhood clubs."

Lakeview YMCA
3333 North Marshfield Avenue
773-248-3333

Much more than you'd expect, with a four lane pool, cardio and weight rooms, and racquetball courts.

Irving Park YMCA
4251 West Irving Park Road
773-777-7500

Indoor heated pool and loads of classes.

Chicago Area Runners Association
www.cararuns.org
312-666-9836

CARA offers training programs, discounts on runs throughout the area, running clubs, and plenty of social events.

Absolutely Free in Chicago

Grant Park
From Randolph Street to Roosevelt Road, between Michigan Avenue and the lakefront, Grant Park has over 300 acres to explore, including tennis courts and softball fields.

Lakefront Running Path
Runs from the northernmost part of Lincoln Park South through Grant Park and down to the Museum of Science and Technology in Hyde Park— an eighteen mile trip. Check at www.cararuns.org to find a trail map, plus distances.

Lincoln Park
From North Avenue to West Hollywood Avenue, between Lake Shore Drive and Clark Avenue, this park has space for biking, rollerblading, running, softball, and kickball. There's even a chess pavilion. Cross-country skiers can also be found here in the winter. The stretch between Fullerton and Irving Park has exercise stations along the path.

Los Angeles

The Equestrian

Griffith Park Horse Rentals

Los Angeles Equestrian Center
480 Riverside Drive (in the Los Angeles Equestrian Center)
Burbank, CA
818-840-8401 / 818-840-9063

Sunset Stables
3400 North Beachwood Drive
Hollywood, CA
323-464-9612

Bar S. Stables
1850 Riverside Drive
Glendale, CA
818-242-8443

J.P. Stables
1914 Mariposa Street
Burbank, CA
818-843-9890

The Tiger

Pitch`n Putts are fun here. They're like mini professional golf courses. You can find them everywhere

Armand Hammer
601 Club View Drive
310-276-1604
$2 for 9 holes

Rahcho Park—3 par Pitch`n Putt
10460 West Pico Boulevard
310-838-7373
$5 for 9 hole Pitch 'n Putt / $5 for a bucket of balls for driving range

The Scavenger

Get yourself to the Long Beach Outdoor Antiques and Collectibles Market at Veterans Stadium in Long Beach, or the Santa Monica Airport Antiques and Collectibles Market.
www.longbeachantiquemarket.com

The Bounty Hunter

Los Angeles Gun Club
1375 East 6th Street
213-612-0931
Facilities include indoor pistol, indoor rifle and archery ranges.

The Chef

Bristol Farms Cooking School
www.bristolfarms.com
1570 Rosecrans Avenue

Manhattan Beach, CA
310-233-4752

Demo classes on a variety of cuisines offered in the evenings range in price from $25 to $35 per person.

Hip Cooks
www.hipcooks.com
672 South Avenue 21, Unit 5
Los Angeles, CA

Small classes with a variety of themes, such as: "Turning Japanese," "Hot Soup Focus Group," "I Ain't No Turkey," "Autumn in Paris," and "Healthy Fresh and Zingy," with an emphasis on entertaining, held in a loft downtown.

The New School of Cooking
www.newschoolofcooking.com
8690 Washington Boulevard
Culver City, CA
310-842-9702

Offers recreational classes for all levels as well as part time professional cooking and baking programs for around $75.

The Shopper

The L.A. Fashion District
www.fashiondistrict.org
110 East 9th Street, Ste. A-1175
213-488-1153

Located roughly between Main St. and Wall St., you'll find a lot of great stuff here.

Boutiques on Melrose Avenue between La Brea and Fairfax Avenues.
Lots of trendy stores line this street. Just walk around and browse. Also, there are a lot of fun shops along Sunset Boulevard between Sanborn Avenue and in Silver Lake. Larchmont Village (between Beverly Boulevard and 1st Street) is another good place to stroll.

California Market Center
www.californiamarketcenter.com
110 East 9th Street
213-630-3600

Offers seasonal shows and even has permanent vendors. Can be hit or miss, but worth a shot on a rainy afternoon.

The Exercise Freak

24 Hour Fitness
www.24hourfitness.com

One of the cheaper gyms in town with branches everywhere. Make sure you sign up for the free trial!

Yoga Works
www.yogaworks.com
1426 Montana Avenue, 2nd Floor
Santa Monica, CA
310-393-5150
2215 Main Street
Santa Monica, CA
310-393-5150
1256 Westwood Boulevard
Westwood
310-234-1200

Center for Yoga
230 1/2 North Larchmont Boulevard
Los Angeles
323-464-1276

YMCA Los Angeles
www.ymcala.org
Here are a few of the larger branches:
Downtown:
    401 South Hope Street
    213-624-2348
Hollywood:
    1553 North Schrader Boulevard
    323-467-4161
Westside:
    11311 La Grange Avenue
    310-477-1511

Absolutely Free in L.A.

Topanga Canyon State Park
Miles of beautiful trails for hiking and biking.

The beach
This one's a no-brainer. Some special spots include Zuma Beach in Malibu and Leo Carillo State Beach, just before the Ventura County line.

Griffith Park
Over fifty miles of hiking and biking trails, plus picnic areas, tennis courts, a golf course, and playgrounds.

Runyon Canyon Park
2000 North Fuller Avenue
Just a few blocks from Hollywood Boulevard, you'll find hiking trails, a dog park, and get your fill of star sightings.

Venice Beach
Miles of path both on and off the beach.

Miami

The Equestrian

Ascot Farm
12335 SW 46 Street
305-559-7868

The Tiger

Palmetto Golf Course
9300 SW 152nd Street
305-238-2922

Open until 9 p.m. so try the driving range at night!
$6 large bucket / $3.75 small bucket

The Bounty Hunter

Trail Glades Range, Inc.
17650 SW 8th Street
305-226-1823

Outdoor pistol (25 and 50 yards), outdoor rifle, trap and skeet shooting.

The Chef

Chef Allen's
www.chefallens.com
19088 NE 29th Avenue
Aventura
305-935-2900

Starting at $50 a person, Chef Allen offers classes such as Tropical, Latin,
and Caribbean Cooking; New World Cuisine; and Exotic Cuisines of the
Mediterranean.

The Exercise Freak

Crunch Fitness
www.crunch.com
1259 Washington Avenue
Miami Beach, FL
305-674-8222

Offers a variety of interesting classes such as Cardio Striptease and
Kama Sutra. This is a chain, with gyms in Atlanta, New York, Chicago, San
Francisco, Boston and Los Angeles. I list it here because it's one of the
better ones in Miami for the money.

Absolutely Free in Miami

The beach, of course.

Old Cutler Bike Path

Old Cutler Road from SW 72nd Street to SW 224th Street
305-375-1647

Hop on for a scenic ride to lots of hotspots.

Snapper Creek Bikeway

SW 117th Avenue from SW 16th Street to / SW 107th Avenue and SW 72nd Street
305-375-1647

Ride along the waterway and then stop at the Snapper Creek Park.

New York City

The Equestrian

Claremont Riding Academy

89th Street and Amsterdam Avenue
212-724-5100

Kensington Stables

www.kensingtonstables.com
51 Caton Place
Brooklyn, NY
718-972-4588

The Tiger

Chelsea Piers Golf Club

www.chelseapiers.com
212-336-6400
23rd Street and the Hudson River

A fun place to hit balls overlooking the Hudson River. $20 will get you approximately 90 balls (depending on what time you go). Call for weekly specials.

The Scavenger

Take the Metro North train to Hudson, Tarrytown or Croton. You'll get lost in treasures. The fall is the best time of year to do this. Or, if you want to stay local, go to the Antiques Market on 6th Avenue and 26th Street in Manhattan. It's only open on the weekends, so go early to see the best stuff!

The Bounty Hunter

West Side Pistol Range
20 West 20th Street
212-243-9448

$54 will get you a private lesson on firearm safety with an instructor, a .22 rifle, and fifty rounds of ammo. Cool leather outfit sold separately.

The Chef

Grandma's Secrets
www.grandmasecrets.com
640 West 138th Street
212-862-8117

Learn how to make sensational pies such as banana cream, coconut, or lemon meringue for less than $50 a class. Grandma will also come to your home and do parties or individual lessons.

Cooking by the Book
www.cookingbythebook.com
11 Worth Street
212-966-9799

For around $100 (a little more pricey), you can choose from a variety of courses ranging from seasonal cooking to wine and urban lifestyle dishes.

Cooking by Heart
www.cookingbyheart.com
203-629-1831

Offers guided tasting parties in New York City and Connecticut for around $35 per person. A great idea for a group! Private cooking classes are a bit more.

The Shopper

Century 21
22 Cortlandt Street (between Church and Broadway, downtown)
212-227-9092

This place is a zoo. But it's got everything from shoes to sheets at amazing prices.

H & M
The big one is on 50th Street and Madison Avenue, but there are others around the city.

Here you'll find Euro-style fashions dirt cheap. Think of them of the IKEA of fashion. You can find these in Baltimore, Chicago, Philadelphia, Washington, D.C., and Boston, just to name a few!

Loftworks
100 Lafayette Street
212-343-8088

Offers a good selection of chic clothes at reasonable prices. Can be hit or miss at times.

New York Sample Sales

Log onto www.nysale.com and sign up for a free emailed listing of weekly sales from well-known designers. Going to a sample sale is a real trip. You'll fall over half naked ladies trying on clothes, and you may even get into a fight with someone who tries to steal your bargain. This is especially true at the Barneys New York Warehouse Sale. But it's all part of the game!

Fine & Klein
119 Orchard Street
212-674-6720

Your mouth'll water over these designer handbags. Though sold at a deep discount, you can still wind up spending a bundle. Fun to visit, as it's located on the Lower East Side. Stop at Katz's Deli afterwards for a fat corned beef sandwich, the other half of which you'll fit in your phat handbag.

Loehmanns
www.loehmanns.com
7th Avenue between 16th and 17th Streets
212-352-0856
(and the original in Riverdale)
5740 Broadway
718-543-6420

Though many complain that it's "not as good as it used to be," you can still get a great deal here on basics for work, such as suits and coats, not to mention shoes and handbags. And even if you don't live in NYC, there are Loehmann's Plazas all over the U.S.

The Exercise Freak

Lenox Hill Neighborhood House
www.lenoxhill.org
70th Street between 1st and 2nd Avenues

One of the best bargain gyms in NYC. A small weight room, but it has a great pool. Fees are dirt cheap.

Dolphin Fitness Clubs
www.dolphinfitnessclubs.com

These bare bones gyms are open 24 hours in select locations around NYC (mostly on the East Side).

McBurney YMCA
125 West 14th Street
212-741-9210

Offers classes galore as well as a huge pool. You'll pay less here than at most NYC gyms.

Absolutely Free in NYC

Hudson River Parks
Recently extended, this path now stretches all the way from Battery Park to beyond the George Washington Bridge on the west side of Manhattan. There are also kayaking and rowing piers along the way.

Central Park
More beautiful than ever before, you can spend the day rollerblading, biking, horseback riding, jogging, hiking, boating, or just laying in the grass of this 800+ acre oasis in the middle of New York City.

East River Walk
Follow this path all the way from 63rd Street along the East River up to the 120s. Stop at John Jay Park, Carl Schurz Park, and even Gracie Mansion, once home to many NYC mayors, but now a historic city site.

San Francisco

The Tiger

Mission Bay Golf Center
1200 6th Street
415-431-7888

$8 for a bucket

The Scavenger

San Francisco Design and Antique Mall
www.sfantique.com
701 Bayshore Boulevard

Over 200 vendors with a variety of merchandise.

The Bounty Hunter

Pacific Rod & Gun Club
520 John Muir Drive
415-586-8349

Indoor rifle, trap, skeet, sporting clays and archery

The Chef

City College of San Francisco
Fort Mason Art Campus
www.ccsf.edu (click on Educational Programs and their Continuing Education section)
Laguna & Marina Blvd—Bldg B
415-561-1860

With topics like Rustic Italian Cooking, Exotic Vietnamese Desserts, or We Be Sushi for under $50 each, who could go wrong?

The Shopper

Crossroads Trading Post

1901 Fillmore Street
415-775-8885
1409 Fifth Street
Berkeley, CA
510-559-9600

Thumb through used clothing in great condition, plus a few pieces from wholesalers. They'll also buy clothing, but don't bring your old Gap stuff from 1998—they're very picky!

Buffalo Exchange
1555 Haight Street
415-431-7733

Castoff clothing of the hippest labels in the middle of the Haight-Ashbury scene.

The Exercise Freak

San Francisco YMCA
www.ymcasf.org
Ten branches offer fitness centers at lower costs than standard gyms in the area. Find the one nearest you online.

Absolutely Free in San Francisco

Golden Gate Promenade
415-561-4323

For a popular run or walk, head to the promenade, which runs three miles through Marina Green, Crissy Field, the Presidio, and finally to the Golden Gate Bridge.

Seattle

The Tiger

West Seattle Golf Club
www.westseattlegolf.com
4470 35 Avenue SW
206-935-5187

You'll get a great view of the city at this facility. Check out specials online.

The Scavenger

Pioneer Square Antique Mall
www.pioneersquareantiquemall.com
602 First Avenue
206-624-1164
Monday-Saturday 10:30 to 5:30 and Sunday 12:00 to 5:00

Antiques and collectibles abound in this quaint shopping area.

The Bounty Hunter

Roger Dahl Rifle Training Range
4470 35th Avenue SW
206-935-4883

This has airgun only but there are plenty of courses.
Only open during evenings.

The Chef

NuCulinary
www.nuculinary.com
6523 California Avenue SW
206-932-3855

Learn to make authentic Asian soups and roll sushi like the pros for $50.

The Shopper

Red Light
312 Broadway E
206-329-2200
Two packed floors of fun, new, and vintage clothing.

Les Amis
3420 Evanston Avenue E
206-632-4895

Catch a sale at this designer European boutique and you'll walk away looking great for next to nothing.

The Exercise Freak

Downtown Seattle YMCA
www.seattleymca.org
909 4th Avenue
206-382-5010

Washington, D.C.

The Equestrian

Rock Creek Horse Center
www.rockcreekhorsecenter.com
5100 Glover Road
202-362-0117

Wheaton Park Stables
www.wheatonparkstables.com
1101 Glenallan Ave
Wheaton, MD (14 miles outside Washington)
301-622-2424

The Tiger

East Potomac Park Golf Course and Driving Range
www.golfdc.com
1090 Ohio Street SW
202-554-7660

Practice your swing among a view of the Washington Monument, National Airport, the Capital and Washington National Cathedral.

The Bounty Hunter

Prince George's County Trap and Skeet Center
10400 Good Luck Road
Glenn Dale, MD
301-577-7178

Trap and skeet shooting, sporting clays, instruction available.

Gilbert Indoor Range
www.gilbertindoorrange.com
1022 Rockville Pike
Rockville, MD
301-217-0055

You'll spend $145 to take a training course and get certified, but once you are, you'll pay only $29 per day to fire on their range.

The Chef

What's Cooking?
email only: whatsckng@aol.com
1917 S. Street NW

Learn how to cook in a small group in a townhouse kitchen located near Dupont Circle. Fun classes, such as Black Tie Dinner, Morroccan Magic, and Tapas Party, cost $50 per person.

The Shopper

Secondi Consignment Clothing
1611 Connecticut Avenue NW
202-667-1122

Although a little pricier than some, Secondi offers secondhand goods from some designers that range from the Gap to Chanel. Looking to clean out your closet? Consignments are taken on appointment.

Designer Consigner
1919 Pennsylvania Avenue
202-296-2610

High-quality consignment meets vintage wear meets up-and-coming designers at Designer Consigner.

Potomac Mills
www.potomacmills.com
703-643-1855
Prince William, VA

For a real shopping adventure, join the tour buses and the herds migrating to Potomac Mills, the outlet mall of outlet malls. Polo, Banana Republic, Brooks Brothers, Ann Taylor, Abercrombie & Fitch, J.Jill, and Nordstrom Rack are among the hundreds of options available.

Shoe Fly
2618 Wilson Boulevard
Arlington, VA
703-243-6490

Find shoes and handbags from a variety of well-known designers, all priced at under $70.

The Exercise Freak

YMCA National Capital
www.ymcawashdc.org
1711 Rhode Island Avenue, NW
202-862-9622

The National Capital YMCA seems to have it all: a climbing wall, weight room, indoor swimming pool, basketball courts, and an indoor track. No membership required, just sign up for the classes you're interested in.

Montgomery Aquatic Center
5900 Executive Boulevard
Rockville, MD (at the White Flint Metro stop)
301-468-4211
$5.50 county residents, $7.00 non-county

Swimming pool, water slide, 10-meter diving board, saunas, exercise room, racquetball courts all available

Anacostia Fitness Recreation Center
1800 Anacostia Drive SE
202-698-2250

It may not be the prettiest part of town, but the fitness center here offers a monthly membership for $25 and a yearly one for just $125. There's an outdoor pool and tennis courts are available during the summer, with gym facilities and aerobics available indoors.

Rockville Municipal Swim Center
355 Martins Lane
Rockville, MD
240-314-8750

There's both an outdoor and two indoor lap pool at this swim center.

The Thompson Boat Center
2900 Virginia Avenue NW
202-333-9543

Kayaks $8/hour or $24/day
Canoes $8/hour or $22/day
Rowing shells: $13/hour

Absolutely Free in D.C.

C&O Canal Towpath
Built between 1828 and 1850, this 184.5-mile-long trail runs from Georgetown all the way to Cumberland, Maryland. Bikers, joggers, and walkers abound.

Washington and Old Dominion Trail
www.wodfriends.org
703-729-0596

A 45-mile trail built along an old railroad line, it runs through Alexandria, Falls Church, Vienna, and Herndon.

Capital Crescent Trail/Georgetown Branch Trail
202-234-4874

Just over 11 miles of surprisingly varied and scenic trail used for running, biking, and cross-country skiing.

www.bikewashington.org

Find biking trails and biking events at this site dedicated to all things biking in the Washington area.

Stair Running

Try the infamous "Exorcist" stairs at 36th and Prospect in Georgetown, or the Mall steps that lead from the Reflecting Pool to the Abraham Lincoln statue. For a more political approach, run the stairs at the Supreme Court or Library of Congress.

Rock Creek Park
3545 Williamsburg Lane NW

As a break from urban living, head to the city's Rock Creek Park for a 1.5-mile fitness trail, running paths, and 11 miles of bridle trail.

American University Outdoor Tennis Courts
4400 Massachusetts Avenue NW
202-885-3000

Free, on a first-come-first-serve basis.

8

Dating Someone Else

Yes, sooner or later, this will happen too

Just because you've mastered the concept of "dating yourself," doesn't mean you should hole up and avoid trying to meet other people. By now, you're an independent, city-savvy woman, with an address, a job, and health insurance, who knows how to take herself out and have a good time. And for some, that's enough. For others, well, there's just something missing.

Urban Dating

Moving to a big city is the ultimate opportunity to meet a whole slew of interesting people (read: guys). With endless venues, clubs, and social outlets, you don't have to look far to find potential activities (read: guys). Same thing goes for those who're looking to meet women (in addition to or instead of guys). In fact, many people make the move to a city for this reason alone. And if you're one of them, you'll have plenty to choose from, if you know where to look.

That's what's so great about dating in the city. There are as many people with unique interests as there are activities. And not all of them are city-oriented, either. From horseback riders to mountain bikers, cities offer just as many, if not more, opportunities to explore rural interests, too, so sometimes you just need to think outside the box. You'd be amazed at how many people want (and need) to escape city life on the weekends. Many times this is the perfect opportunity to let your guard down and find others who share your interests.

So for those skeptics out there, don't give up! There are good, nice, normal single people everywhere, but—like anything else—finding them may take some work. If you add dating to your list of priorities when you're also looking for an apartment or a job (or both), it may just be a bit too much right now. Wait a bit if you have to. Just don't forget about it later on.

So, Why Haven't You Met Him Yet?

If you're sitting on your couch wondering why you're not meeting someone (and meeting someone is a priority), um, maybe you shouldn't be sitting on your couch. Meeting people takes energy . . . exhaustive energy. Chapters 3 and 4, which focus on finding a job, chasing your dream, and even dealing with rejection, are good ones to reference. Just replace the word "job" with "date" and "job rejection" with "date rejection." And since you're not marrying every single person you date (hopefully), the more you date, the more you'll deal with this little issue. But don't worry, you'll be doing your fair share of rejecting, too!

Being relentless about dating in the same way you would about finding a job or an apartment doesn't necessarily mean you call the same guy 40 times and ask him why he's not calling you back. But it does mean that you don't give up and continue to search in creative ways until the right situation comes along. You're going to have to use a little common sense—or "sechel," as my grandma would say.

One of the best ways to get started is to ask yourself what it is that you like to do. Have you actually ever sat down to figure this out? Think about it. What made you happy as a kid? Are you a theater person? Maybe you can audition for a show. Do you like to sauté shrimp in a duck *confit jus*? If you even know what that means, a cooking class may be in your future. A book club is a fun (and free) way to meet others who enjoy reading. Just make sure you join a club that appeals to both sexes if you're interested in meeting men.

You can even take this whole activity thing a step further. If meeting someone is more important to you than the activity itself, consider signing up for something you would never sign up for otherwise, but one where you know you'll find some prospects. A friend of mine enrolled in a woodworking class to get acquainted with some pretty handy (and sculpted) guys. And let me tell you, she's no Bob Villa. Well, guess what? She's dating one now because she learned to like woodworking pretty darn fast after catching a glimpse of the dudes in her class. Get it? The same goes for scuba, hiking, fly fishing, or metalsmithing—you get the point. And if this sounds too contrived to you, then don't do it. But it has been known to work.

Where to Meet 'Em

There are ways and then there are ways. Like we've talked about before, you can pretty much meet people anywhere, but there are specific venues for this sort of stuff. Here are a few that seem to work, listed in no particular order, so feel free to choose whichever one(s) work best for you:

Network

Ugh. Again with the networking? Yep. Networking is the best way to get anything you want. See chapter 3. Talk to your friends, ask your coworkers. Or surrender and go on one set-up organized by your mom's high school friend. Hey, you never know.

Strategize

Figure out what it is that you're looking for. Does religion matter? If so, it's probably worth signing up for activities offered through religious organizations. Do you need to date someone who lives in town? Then don't get set up with someone who's just in for the weekend, unless you'd consider doing the long-distance thing. Obviously, your strategy may fly out the door if you meet someone on the train who just happens to be visiting from Utah, but hey, nobody said it was an exact science.

Do Stuff

The more places you go, the more people you meet. You're not going to meet someone sitting at home, especially if you're not into online dating. Free classes, films, or weird alternative lectures near the university—just go to something!

If you can't think of anything, try www.8at8.com, a dinner club where four women and four men are paired up based on common interests and backgrounds and then meet up for dinner in a relaxed setting. In D.C., also check out www.dcplay.org, a group made up of 21 to 39-year-olds (mostly single) who meet for dinner, then go to see a play.

Get a Pet

They don't call dogs "Chick Magnets" for nothing. Same works for us chicks, though. Plant yourself and Fido at a dog run or a nearby park and they'll come out in droves (the boys, that is). It's a whole 'nother world out there when you have a pet. In D.C., there's even a "Doggy Happy Hour" at the Adams Mill Bar and Grill (1813 Adams Mill Road NW), where you can mingle with other dog owners over a drink.

Join a Gym

If you didn't already know this, gyms are very social places. And you don't have to be in great shape to meet a guy there, either. Believe me, plenty of great ones aren't sporting six-pack abs, so you don't need to be Pamela Anderson. When you take away the club music and pluck out the few people with the perfect bodies and perfect gym outfits, you're left with the rest of us. And that's still a lot of people with whom you may just connect! If you don't like the "gym scene," try joining a gym at a community center—it'll feel less intimidating and you may find yourself able to strike up a conversation with someone waiting in line for the machine neither of you knows how to use. Oh, and don't wear your headphones if you really want to try this tactic: some guys may think you're not interested in talking. You can find some great gyms listed in chapter 7.

Online Dating

It's not that bad. There really are some winners in cyberspace. If you can deal with the annoying "winks" and "smiles" and quirky little internet lingo reminiscent of the days where you wrote SWAK on the back of a letter at camp, try a few of these. One good thing about online dating: You can weed out a lot of junk simply by reading someone's profile. Of course, some say this goes a bit too far and people become as dispensable as a paper resumé, but it's worth a shot. Hey, nobody said it was an exact science. Oh wait, did I already say that? As far as which ones to use? There are too many to mention, but the biggies are www.match.com, www.lavalife.com, and www.jdate.com (for Jewish singles). You can also engage in "online networking" (a form of dating, just packaged differently) at www.friendster.com and www.myspace.com.

Dating Services

This is kind of like a headhunter that you pay upfront. You let someone else do all the legwork for you and then, allegedly, you meet the person of your dreams. Does it work? Sometimes. Is it worth the money? Sometimes. What does that mean? I don't know. But it's worth investigating. Some interesting ones include Drip Café (www.dripcafe.com), more of a hybrid dating service that also lists a variety of eclectic cafes in New York and Boston where you can get set up while devouring a freshly baked scone. There's also It's Just Lunch (www.itsjustlunch.com), which gets people together for . . . well, lunch.

Speed Dating

Heard of it? Tried it? Down a few shots (okay, maybe that's a bad idea)—but grab a friend and go. Have you been through sorority rush? Well, it's just like that, except you may wind up with a boyfriend. You get anywhere from three to eight minutes with someone before the bell rings and you're herded off to the next table. For some, this is a dream come true. Why endure dinner and drinks when three minutes'll give you just enough time to learn everything about the guy? If you're lucky, you may even catch his first *and* last name! Try these: www.8minutedating.com, www.hurrydate.com, or www.fastdater.com.

Go to Grad School

Long for the days where college coeds ran in the quad throwing Frisbees with their shirts off? It was so safe then, so easy to meet people, hookup and then, well, move on. So, if you're considering a job change, why not consider graduate school, too? Putting yourself in an academic environment with other people like yourself may just give you more exposure to potential mates. Some companies even pay tuition reimbursement!

Bars

I know it's not the romantic story you want to tell at your rehearsal dinner, but there are so many kinds of bars with all types of music (and even activities), that there are sure to be people like you who frequent these places. Even if you don't like bars, you can try to find some that appeal to your musical tastes or interests, as opposed to those where you just slink in and light up. Big cities offer everything from board game bars to country music to my all-time favorite, karaoke! And believe me, anyone who's willing to make a fool out of himself at a karaoke bar is good enough for me!

What to Do with Him Once You've Spotted Him

You saw him, you liked him, you actually talked to him at the basketball game. Now what?

How to Ask Someone Out

You're happening. You've got a job. You even have a place to live. So how come you can't pick up the phone and ask someone out? It all goes back to chapter 3: rejection. Seems like it's taking over this book, doesn't it? When it comes to asking someone out, you have absolutely *nothing* to lose. If he says no, you are uncomfortable for about a minute, and then you're in the same boat you were in two minutes before. So call the dude and say, "Hey, want to do something this weekend?" It's that simple. And yes, if you ask him out, you should pay.

How to Blow Someone Off

We've all done this. And there's really no right way to do it. It's worse when someone does it to us. You don't want to see him anymore? Don't call him back. He'll get it. If you're one of those "nice types" who has to explain, then answer your phone and just say you're not feeling it, you don't know why. Don't make any other statement about him, your compatibility, or specifics about your date from hell. Come to think of it, just don't call back. He'll get it.

How to Look Cool Standing by the Bar

If you're standing by the bar wondering how to look cool standing by the bar, let's face it, you probably don't. You either need to not care (and then you *will* look cool), or just get over the fact that you aren't cool. If you're anything like me, you'll fit into the latter category, which means that after about four minutes you wonder why the heck you came into the bar in the first place and you leave. Pajamas and a huge bowl of buttered popcorn are a much better choice, don't you think? Yeah, I'm with you.

How to Pass Someone over to a Friend Without Seeming Like a Jerk

This one's quite the challenge. You meet a nice guy and it's just not happening. But you actually think he'd be better with a friend of yours. How do you tell him this without insulting him? You can do one of two things.

1. Lie. Tell him you're kind of getting more involved with someone else and it's working really well, but you really like him and think he'd hit it off with your friend.

2. Skip part one of that sentence and just tell him you think he'd really hit it off with your friend. It may be awkward for about a minute, but think about how much time you've saved him. I mean, hey, he should be thanking you!

How to Steal Your Friend's Boyfriend

I have no idea.

How to Have a One Night Stand and Not Feel Guilty

This is probably one of the most liberating things a woman on her own can do: hook up with someone and have absolutely no mental connection to that person whatsoever. As long as you're safe, try it. Just don't start getting attached. The way to do this is to find someone you're remotely attracted to but with whom you really have no emotional connection (hint: here's where bars come in handy). If you are 100-percent confident that there's no chance you'll ever be together, it's easier to separate the emotion from the relationship. And that's exactly how a one night stand (or a few of these) can be successful. No emotion—no disappointment. Not for everyone, but for some it's fun.

How to Date Someone at Work

Ooooh, you're treading on thin ice here. This one really depends on your personality. The only thing I can say is that you have to assume either the relationship or your job is probably going to end at some point. You'll have to decide which is more important. Some quick tips to keep in mind if your work romance does blossom: Don't be obvious about it, try not to smooch in front of coworkers, *please* don't date your interns, and, if things do get serious, talk about the next steps (i.e., will you both stay at your company?) before you go public with your romance.

While we're on the subject…

Some notes about THE GAME.

Don't let anyone tell you that dating is not a game—it is a game. The biggest, most strategic game you will ever play! I mean, c'mon, how many times has this happened to me—I mean, you?

You're a sweet, smart, and sexy newcomer to a big city. You meet someone, perhaps through an introduction, or randomly at a party. You've heard of him before, maybe because your friend warned you about him saying he was a player. But he's cute and you're up for a conversation. He's intrigued. You're indifferent because you don't know him. He likes that. Still, your lack of interest makes you...

Mysterious!

He asks you out. You say yes. And why not? You've got nothing to lose. You go to a very nice Moroccan restaurant (that he chose), where he proceeds to ask you details about your life. He listens, he's engaging. You answer his questions, slightly impressed that he pays so much attention to you. But, because you're a smart woman, you're unsure, you don't trust him yet, you hold back. This makes you...

Elusive!

And he really likes that. He can't read you, he can't get a sense of whether or not you're into him, you're holding the reigns ...he's putty in your hands. He looks at you, you say "What?" He says "You're pretty." You like the fact that you're not into him ... yet, but secretly, you're psyched that he's into you. You ask yourself how he got a reputation of being such a player when in fact he's so attentive and kind. He barely touches his food, comments on your barrettes, your belt. My god, he notices your accessories! The man is amazing! But no, you're not into him yet, well ... you're getting there.

Later that same date night: He tries to kiss you, and even though you kind of want to kiss him, too, you pretend that you are not ready and act shy. Now he really likes you. You think.

Next day: He calls you. He had a great time. When can he see you again? Mid-week date? Of course! Wow, he's not too busy. He doesn't spend too much time at work. That's a good sign. You say yes. It's okay for you to say yes because *he likes you.*

See, here's where it gets tricky. You're right on the cusp of falling for him, which could be dangerous, because so far you really haven't cared that much. So now's when your "Player Radar" needs to turn on so that you're prepared for what might happen next.

You plan for sushi on Tuesday.

Wednesday you have Italian.

Thursday you have Greek.

Friday you have Sex.

What? I didn't say anything. Sunday you have brunch. Oooh...

And it hits you. You *do* like him. A lot. You think to yourself, "I finally have a new boyfriend!" You wonder if he's dating anyone else.

Okay, I must cut in here, because we have a small problem. You see, he is not your boyfriend. I know the whole brunch the morning after thing can be misleading, but you must realize that despite this entire litany of dates, it is absolutely 100 percent impossible for a guy who was ever thought of as a player to be your boyfriend in just one week.

Your mistake is that you didn't realize it was his testosterone talking, not him. This was the guy who was held back in kindergarten for being too active — the one who always had on the backwards baseball cap in college and the lacrosse jersey with his name on it from high school. He looks hot after a run, he looks hot reading the paper. He looks hot, because he *is* hot. He was the one who pursued you, took you out, and seemed to be eager to escalate the pace of your budding relationship.

He did this not because he wanted to be your boyfriend (yet), but because he was intrigued and because he was impatient. That is why "he" is a "he." You call him on Monday. Hey, you're progressive. Can he have dinner? Oh, has to work late. Too bad, you're cool. Hmm ... why was he so available last week?

Okay, you'll wait until Thursday. Yes, if he doesn't call you by Thursday, you'll call him. That's enough time to wait, right? Right?

Oh my. This is getting pathetic.

Why?

Because you're planning your entire week around when he might call you! Remember, two weeks ago at this time you didn't even know the guy. You were taking a yoga class, grabbing sushi and a movie, going to the bookstore and perusing until 11:00. You were dating yourself! Did we not just read chapter 7?

A better option, perhaps, would have been not to see him every single night the first week. This is difficult, especially when you're learning about someone in the beginning and he seems so into it. But by taking breaks and not seeing him every night, you're maintaining your own sense of independence, and you're not putting yourself in a position to fall for him so quickly. You're slowing things down before he does.

But you still have time to regain your strong, independent, and elusive self. Do it now before it's too late. Like it or not, the reason he liked you so quickly is because you were a new challenge. Now don't get me wrong, the right guy, of course, isn't going to be this demanding of your strategic energies. But you're not there yet with this guy. You can be yourself, and you should be yourself, but you need to PLAY THE GAME FOR A WHILE.

And really, this means, that you're conducting life as you were when you were independent, and not waiting for someone to call you. You don't want to overload too much at the beginning or you'll lose yourself. You have to assume for at least three months, that he is NOT YOUR BOYFRIEND and you are NOT HIS GIRLFRIEND — and that, for the time being, you can take him or leave him.

Do not call him on Thursday. Do not. Do not. Do not. Very hard to do this, I know.

When he calls you, even if it's a week from Thursday (that's an entire 10 days since you had sex, I mean brunch), you are totally cool. You're now back to step 1.

You're elusive, you're not really that interested anymore.

Now if you get to the point where this is happening after two months (yes, you can hold out for two months like this), bag the guy. He's not worth it. But if you want to keep someone interested, you either have to be naturally able to say "forget it" or pretend that you're able to say "forget it" for at least the first two months of dating.

So you see? It *is* a game. But you can play it. I know you can.

You Found Him!

You finally figure out how to spend your time alone and then, boom, you find him (or her). Why? Because you weren't looking, dummy. You were so busy dating yourself (see Chapter 7) that you forgot to pine. And not pining is a good thing. It's not only a good thing, it's an attractive thing to others. So now that you've found each other, there are places to go and things to see. But because you're living in the city, you're probably still broke, right? And now you'll also have to buy cute little gifts and outfits to wear on your fun dates, so you're really up the creek. The last thing you need is to get evicted after you find the love of your life just because you can't pay your rent!

Which brings us to another point, an aside, if you will: Moving in together after a month to save money? BAD IDEA. Just because you live in an expensive city doesn't mean you shack up with your current fling to save money on your rent. What you do a year or two down the road is your call. But don't give up your place (and your own life) until you know he's "the one." And typically you don't know this for at least six months. I said at least! (Note to any moms reading this section: it's a different generation.)

Cheap and Unique Dating Spots

Dating really doesn't have to be expensive. Sure, a Broadway show, two cab rides, and dinner will cost close to $200, but who said you had to do that? Save it for when your parents come to town. Options, my friend, options. There are plenty of other choices that are cheap, cheap, cheap or free, free, free. Plus, you'll look all the more creative if you're not suggesting "dinner and a movie" *again*. C'mon, you're more interesting than that, aren't you? Aren't you?

"What Do You Want to Do?" "I Don't Know, What Do You Want to Do?"

With local publications covering just about every event, restaurant, bar, concert, tour, museum, etc., out there, it's hard to complain about having nothing to do. Still, how many times have you been sitting in your downtown apartment—smack in the middle of all of the action—and feel like you have absolutely nothing to do? Me, too.

Dating will quickly get you out of that mode. You'll have to think creatively if you want to impress, or if you want to find something different. So, wherever you live, grab a city guide or entertainment supplement of your daily paper. Most are geared for twenty- and thirty-somethings anyway. They pretty much list everything you'd want to do and then some. Make sure to check out the listings at the end of the chapter. Of course, feel free to also use the solo dating suggestions listed in chapter 7 as your dating spots as well. But here are a few other options to try:

See a Student Talent Showcase

Generally, big cities are home to lots of talented people. You got your Broadway types in New York, your TV types in L.A. and your comedy types in Chicago. So call up any acting school in town and find out when their students are offering a talent showcase. From comedies to musicals to dramatic scenes, you'll either discover some amazing stuff or laugh so hard at the poor display of talent. Either way, you're sure to have a good time without spending too much money.

Take an Architecture Tour

This is a fun ways to get to know your own city. Join up with a walking tour listed in the events section of your local paper or read up on the style of the buildings and do your own.

Eat Breakfast Instead of Dinner

Let's compare bills here for, say, pancakes and eggs versus chicken and potatoes (and alcohol). Hmmm. . . I think it's safe to say that you'll save a lot of money if you suggest going out for breakfast instead of dinner.

Tour an Art Museum

Most universities let you in their museums for free. Also, many cities have smaller galleries with relatively inexpensive entrance fees, but fabulous (albeit small) exhibits. See the listings at the end of the chapter.

Go to Outdoor Concerts

Get lawn seats at any outdoor amphitheater. Why spend $75 when you can spend $15 for nosebleeds? Think of it as live radio. Instead of an expensive concert ticket, grab a gourmet meal to go and have a picnic in the park. Or just make peanut butter and jelly sandwiches and bring a box of Oreos.

Rent a Movie

From the library. Yep, they're free. Don't expect anything too steamy though.

Register for Restaurant.com

Online coupons come in handy, especially when you're paying. One word of advice: Don't use this on a first date—you'll look really cheap. But if it's your second or third? Show him your true colors and sign up for the free online dining program at www.restaurant.com. You'll get major discounts at hundreds of eateries nationwide in the form of downloadable gift certificates, with many offering $25 certificates for only $10. For that price, two can certainly eat for one. Make sure to check out the fine print, as some aren't valid on weekends and may not include alcohol.

Cook Together

If going out to dinner is not interesting to you, try cooking a meal together. It's fun (and can be very sexy). If you need a little help, see the inexpensive cooking schools listed in chapter 7.

People-Watch

Won't cost you a dime. Plop yourself anywhere. My favorite is going to Grand Central Terminal in NYC during rush hour when I have nowhere to go, and watching the expressions of people who are late for their trains. Another fun place to do this is at street fairs or craft festivals.

Sit on a Stoop

Some of my best dates have been sitting on a stoop with an ice cream cone engaged in a deep conversation. All the money in the world spent on extracurricular activities can't replace the spark of two people connecting. You'll know it if you feel it.

Some Final Thoughts on Dating

I really hesitated to write this because it seems so, well, cheesy. But it's true, so I'll go ahead. Don't get discouraged if you don't find the love of your life in your twenties or thirties. It's worth holding out for the right person rather than settling. Because as exciting as planning a wedding is, it's what comes after that really matters.

So hang in there and realize that you've got to kiss a lot of frogs first.

City-Specific Dating Resources

Atlanta

Newspapers Geared toward Twenty and Thirtysomethings

AccessAtlanta (www.accessatlanta.com)

Sunday Paper (www.sundaypaper.com)

Creative Loafing (www.creativeloafing.com)

Places to Go

Piedmont Park
www.piedmontpark.org

From "Bark in the Park" to "Screen on the Green" and free Atlanta Symphony Orchestra concerts, there's a lot happening at this newly renovated (and magnificent) park in midtown.

Churchill Grounds
www.churchillgrounds.com
660 Peachtree Street
404-876-3030

Plenty of live jazz to keep the night going. You'll get the best deals Monday through Wednesday, when admission and drink minimums are half price.

Venture Value Cinema
3750 Venture Drive
Duluth, GA

Smooch all you want for $1.99 in this vintage movie theater (heck, for this price, you can even see films so bad you walked out on the preview).

Dad's Garage Theater
280 Elizabeth Street
404-523-3141

Watch some very funny people for around $10.

Boston

Newspapers Geared toward Twenty and Thirtysomethings

Boston Phoenix (www.bostonphoenix.com)

Weekly Dig (www.weeklydig.com)

Places to Go

New England Conservatory
www.newenglandconservatory.edu
290 Huntington Avenue
617-585-1100

This beautiful venue offers over 100 free concerts a year, often featuring the world's premier classical musicians.

New England Aquarium
www.neaq.org
Central Wharf
617-973-5200

Explore the deep blue sea at the largest attraction in Boston, over 200,000 gallons of it. Crowded, yes, but still a great date spot. The aquarium also offers reasonably priced whale watching trips, too.

Museum of Bad Art
www.museumofbadart.org
Dedham Community Theater
580 High Street
781-326-0409

Located eight miles from downtown Boston in Dedham, MOBA boasts a "renowned" collection of atrocious art, excavated carefully by loyal volunteers, complete with hysterical narratives. If you can't bear the sight of the works, just catch a movie instead upstairs in the theater.

Harvard University Museums
www.artmuseums.harvard.edu
32 Quincy Street
Cambridge, MA
617-495-9400

Admission is only $6.50 ($5 for students), but is free on Saturday mornings.

Hatch Shell
Esplanade

This is the ultimate spot to be on July 4th. Here you'll catch an incredible display of fireworks while listening to the Boston Pops . . . for free. There are plenty of other events held here, too, usually in the summer and fall.

Newberry Street Galleries

A fun way to spend the afternoon is perusing the high-end shops and art galleries. Stop by any one of the numerous outdoor cafes along this tree-lined district and end your date at the Public Gardens.

Boston Duck Tours
www.bostonducktours.com

Tours depart from the Museum of Science and the Prudential Center in Boston's Back Bay, from March to November. This is a fun way to be a tourist in your own town. Take a land-sea duck tour of Boston in an amphibious vehicle and laugh at how stupid you must look to the people watching you go by. Actually, you'll learn a lot about Boston's rich history and get a great view of the city.

Absolutely Free in Boston

With its historic landmarks, cobblestone streets, and relatively small size, Boston is the perfect city for strolling and exploring. You can wander gorgeous Beacon Hill, meander down the gas-lit Marlborough Street in the Back Bay, or walk the Freedom Trail, passing fascinating sites from Boston's rich history. End your walk in the old-world Italian neighborhood of the North End, where countless family-owned restaurants offer incomparable Italian meals and colorful festivals abound, making you feel like you're in Italy, especially during the feast days, which occur weekends in July and August.

Chicago

Newspapers Geared toward Twenty and Thirtysomethings

Red Eye (www.redeyechicago.com)

Red Streak (www.chicagoredstreak.com)

New City Chicago (www.newcitychicago.com)

Metromix (online only at www.metromix.com)

Chicago Reader (www.chireader.com)

Places to Go

Grant Park

Tuesday nights in the summer, grab a blanket and a bottle of wine and head to Grant Park to watch a movie on the big screen. Check www.metromix.com for schedules.

Vic Theatre
www.brewview.com
3145 North Sheffield
773-929-7150

Get here early to grab a sofa seat; the theatre offers $5 movies during the week when there's not a live concert. Beer and pizza are available—what more could you want?

Ravinia
www.ravinia.com
847-266-5100

From the ease of taking the Metra there to the $10 to $20 lawn seats, Ravinia, just north of Chicago, makes for a fun way to spend an evening. Spread out a picnic and then recline and relax—you can't really see the performers from the lawn, anyhow.

When the cold sets in and the tourists stop coming, Chicago's museums open up for free days:

Absolutely Free in Chicago

Monday Adler Planetarium, Field Museum, Shedd Aquarium, Museum of Science & Industry, Chicago Historical Society

Tuesday Adler Planetarium, Field Museum, Shedd Aquarium, Museum of Science & Industry, Chicago Historical Society, The Art Institute, Museum of Contemporary Art, Swedish American Museum

Wednesday Clarke House Museum, Glessner House Museum

Thursday Chicago Children's Museum, Peggy Notebaert Nature Museum

Friday Spertus Museum

Sunday DuSable Museum of African American History

Los Angeles

Newspapers Geared toward Twenty and Thirtysomethings

Los Angeles City Beat (www.lacitybeat.com)
LA Weekly (www.laweekly.com)

Places to Go

Hollywood Bowl
www.hollywoodbowl.com
2301 North Highland Avenue
Hollywood, CA
323-850-2000

Concerts of all sorts (classical, jazz, and world music especially) six nights a week between June and September, with tickets as low as $1 and $5. Great place for a picnic, whether you make it yourself or buy it there. Romantic for two or fun with a group.

Huntington Library, Art Collections, and Botanical Gardens
www.huntington.org
1151 Oxford Road
San Marino, CA
626-405-2100

Here you'll find 150 beautiful acres of gardens divided by theme: there's a Rose Garden, Shakespeare and Herb Gardens, a Desert Garden, a Japanese Garden, an Australian Garden, Subtropical and Jungle Gardens, a Palm Garden. There are also art exhibitions—usually pretty good ones—and a charming little tea room. (Reservations are required for the tea room: 626-683-8131).

The Getty Museum
www.getty.edu
1200 Getty Center Drive
310-440-7300

A great place for a "getting to know you" sort of date: galleries and gardens for strolling, several cafes, and one nicer restaurant for dining. They also have lots of musical performances, film screenings, lectures, and other events.

Los Angeles County Museum of Art
www.lacma.org
5905 Wilshire Boulevard
323-857-6000

Free jazz on Friday nights and great film screenings every weekend, in addition to exhibitions and a nice restaurant.

American Cinematheque at the Egyptian Theater
www.egyptiantheatre.com
6712 Hollywood Boulevard
323-461-2020

There's always something interesting screening here, and there are lots of bars and restaurants nearby for post-film discussion. Try Boardners (1652 N. Cherokee Avenue), the Pig N' Whistle (6714 Hollywood Boulevard), or Musso and Franks (6667 Hollywood Boulevard)—all which are venerable Hollywood landmarks.

Hollywood Forever Cemetery
6000 Santa Monica Boulevard.
Hollywood, CA
323-469-1181

A group called Cinespia screens old movies outdoors here in the summer, people bring picnics and sit on the grass (not on top of the graves). It's a lot of fun and very L.A.

Silverlake Wine
www.silverlakewine.com
2395 Glendale Boulevard
323-662-9024

A very cool new shop run by several very passionate wine lovers; they hold tastings several times a week, ranging from $10 to 20.

The Wine House
www.winehouse.com (click on Annex homepage)
2311 Cotner Avenue
310-479-3731

They offer Friday night tastings for $20 and a wide range of classes, $40 and up.

Miami

Newspapers Geared toward Twenty and Thirtysomethings

Miami New Times (www.miaminewtimes.com)

Places to Go

Bass Museum
2121 Park Avenue
Miami Beach, FL
305-673-7530

Stroll through the Bass on your second date, after you get fried at the beach on your first. You won't be disappointed by the collection of art.

Rubell Family Collection
95 NW 29th Street
305-573-6090

An impressive collection of contemporary and pop art housed in a former Drug Enforcement Agency warehouse.

Lincoln Road
at 16th Street

Stroll the trendy shops and galleries or grab a drink along this pedestrian-friendly strip.

Vizcaya Museum
3251 South Miami Avenue
305-250-9133

Enlighten yourself (and your date) about the Italian influence on Miami's history by touring this decadent mansion and extensive gardens, built in 1916.

New York City

Newspapers Geared toward Twenty and Thirtysomethings

Village Voice (www.villagevoice.com)

New York Press (www.nypress.com)

www.newyorkled.com (online only—lists free and cheap events happening all over the five boroughs of New York City)

Places to Go

www.audienceextras.com

If you're a theater buff, you may want to consider signing up for this program. For an initial fee of $115 and $85-a-year dues, you can get tickets to art exhibits, theater events, and other shows for less than $5. You may not always get the hottest show in town, but you'll be sure to see some unique theater or music and may get the occasional hit show, depending on availability. Also try www.broadwaybox.com for discount codes and last minute deals.

The Cloisters at Fort Tryon Park

Take the A Train to 190th Street and transfer to the M4 bus going north for one stop. You'll find yourself at one of the most picturesque spots in the city and you'll feel about as far away from traffic as possible.

Upright Citizens Brigade Theater

307 West 26th Street
212-366-9176

See some very funny comedy sketch improv shows (and classes) that won't break your wallet.

Boat Basin at 79th Street

In Riverside Park (79th Street and Riverside Drive)
Grab a drink in a pretty setting overlooking the Hudson River, or bike up the path from Battery City and end your date here.

Free NYC Museums

Guggenheim Museum Soho

575 Broadway at Prince Street
212-423-3500

Fashion Institute of Technology

Resource Center
7th Avenue between 27th and 28th Streets
212-217-5800

National Museum of the American Indian
One Bowling Green
212-668-6624

Art Galleries in Chelsea

Stroll along 9th and 10th Avenues in the 20s on the west side of Manhattan, home to some pretty fascinating artists' lofts and galleries.

Metropolitan Museum of Art
www.metmuseum.org
5th Avenue and 82nd Street
212-535-7710

Okay, there is a "suggested donation," but it *is* a suggestion, and there's no better place for a drink than on the roof garden.

Museum of Sex
www.museumofsex.org
233 5th Avenue
212-689-6337

What better place to go on a third date? Yeah, you know what I'm talking about. Charges admission.

San Francisco

Newspapers Geared toward Twenty and Thirtysomethings

San Francisco Bay Guardian (www.sfbg.com)

SF Weekly (www.sfweekly.com)

Places to Go

Sonoma Valley

Forget the more expensive country of Napa and head to Sonoma Valley, where almost all of the wine tastings are free and many wines can be had for $10 or less. Check out www.sonomavalley.com for more information.

The Parkway Theatre
www.picturepubpizza.com
1834 Park Boulevard
Oakland, CA
510-814-2400

Billed as "California's First Speakeasy Theatre," the Parkway offers cheap movies and semicomfortable couches, plus beer and pizza. Movies are $5 daily and—if you really need to save money—don't miss "two-for-one" Wednesdays.

Seattle

Newspapers Geared toward Twenty and Thirtysomethings

Seattle Weekly (www.seattleweekly.com)

Places to Go

Seattle Art Museum
www.seattleartmuseum.org
100 University Street
206-625-8900

Free admission on first Thursdays of the month.

Ladies Musical Club
www.lmcseattle.org
Offers a free classical music concert series at venues all over Seattle, including the Seattle Art Museum, Asian Art Museum, Frye Art Museum, and Public Library.

Ballard Locks
www.nws.usace.army.mil/opdiv/lwsc
Northwest 54th Street and 32nd Avenue Northwest
206-783-7059

It's mesmerizing to watch the boats pass through the locks. Also check out the fish ladder and see salmon swimming upstream!

Seattle Repertory Theatre
www.seattlerep.org
155 Mercer Street
206-443-2222

Two theaters feature everything from dramas to comedy improv. Offers a "pay what you can" program for selected shows the day of the performance. To be notified, sign up for the e-newsletter on their website.

Washington, D.C.

Newspapers Geared toward Twenty and Thirtysomethings

Sunday Source (www.washingtonpost.com)

Places to Go

Smithsonian Institute
www.si.edu
202-633-1000

With sixteen free museums, the Smithsonian Institute can't be beat for a cheap date. Try the Arthur M. Sackler Gallery (1050 Independence Avenue SW, 202-357-4880), the Freer Gallery of Art (12th Street and Jefferson Drive SW, 202-357-2700), National Air and Space Museum (7th Street and Independence Avenue, 202-357-2700), or the National Postal Museum, which is much more entertaining than you'd think. (2 Massachusetts Avenue NE, 202-633-1000).

Mary Pickford Theater
Library of Congress
James Madison Memorial Building
101 Independence Avenue SE
202-707-5677

Watch free films sponsored by the Library of Congress at this theater several days a week. The theater shows films from the Library's collection, including obscure films, classics, and cult favorites. Reservations are required, as seating is limited.

Carter Barron Amphitheatre
4850 Colorado Avenue NW
202-426-0486

During the summer months, head to the amphitheatre for free concerts, Shakespeare Theatre's Free for All, and other performing artists.

National Zoo
www.nationalzoo.si.edu
3001 Connecticut Avenue
202-673-4800

You can't beat a free zoo for a first (or second, or third) date.

Arlington Cinema 'N' Drafthouse
2903 Columbia Pike
Arlington, VA
703-486-2345

Watch movies in loungey seats for $4.99 while drinking beer and munching on popcorn, or, if you're hungrier, sandwiches and pizza.

Ticketplace
www.ticketplace.org
202-TIC-KETS
407 Seventh Street NW

Check the website or call to find half-priced tickets to Washington-area shows.

U.S. National Arboretum
www.usna.usda.gov/
3501 New York Avenue NE
202-245-2726

Stroll hand-in-hand through your choice of the over 400 acres of trees, bushes, bonsais, and herbs at the arboretum.

And So...

It's a lot of information, I know. But there's so much more to write, so much more to research, so much more to explore. I barely feel as if I've skimmed the surface. I hope this book has given you a few of the tools you need to take the next step in whatever it is you're looking to do with your life. It's okay if you don't know exactly how things will unfold. That's the beauty of taking a risk. Learn to laugh at yourself, take chances, and—every now and then—get out of line. Hey, someone's got to make it—why shouldn't it be you? Good luck!

For new information and additional resources to help you make it in the city, log on to www.makingitinthecity.com. Be sure to send in your suggestions, too. After all, your advice is what helps create the ultimate list of insider info for women making it in the city all over!

About the Author

Adina Kalish Neufeld is an author/lecturer who writes and speaks about consumer-oriented survival issues for twenty- and thirtysomethings. Foolishly determined to make life tolerable in the most expensive city in the nation, she moved to New York in 1993 to pursue her passion of writing and happily survived there for over ten years. She has since produced for ABC Television, written for the *New York Times*, the *Atlanta Journal-Constitution*, *USA Today*, *Glamour*, and *Mademoiselle* magazines, as well as for numerous corporate clients.

Adina has a B.A. from Washington University in St. Louis and an M.A. from Syracuse University's Newhouse School of Public Communications. More impressive than her degrees, she has never paid a fee for an apartment, has held more internships than she cares to admit, spends entire weekends perusing Target, and enjoys taking herself out on dates on a regular basis. From working as a toy dog at trade shows to building her own wall to convert a one-bedroom apartment into two, she doles out only tried and true advice that she herself has lived by while starting out in the big city. After conquering New York, she currently resides in Atlanta, where her living space can actually fit more than two people at a time.

Index

W

Washington, D.C.